IN-HOUSE TEA[M]

Editor: Mike Tol[...]

Features editor:

Senior editorial [...]

Editorial and pro[...]

Editorial assistance: Anton Tweedale, Claire Gardiner, Kelsey Strand-Polyak, Katy Georgiou

Designer: Sarah Winter

Design assistance: Caitlin Kenney, Sara Gramner

Picture research: Alex Amend

Production consultant: Iain Leslie

Web editor: Cameron J Macphail

National ad sales: Sue Ostler, Zee Ahmad

Local ad sales: Rob Osborne

Distribution: Nativeps

Financial controller: Sharon Evans

Managing director: Ian Merricks

Publisher: Itchy Group

© 2007 Itchy Group

ISBN: 978-1-905705-17-7

Photography: Tim Ireland, Chris Grossmeier, Joe Millson, Juliet Hookey, Jemima Garthwaite, Karen Jeffrey, Dorrottya Verses, Mario Alberto, Selma Yalazi Dawani, Bas Driessen, Alex Amend

Illustrations: Tom Denbigh, Si Clark, Joly Braime
Cover illustration: Si Clark (www.si-clark.co.uk)

Itchy Group
White Horse Yard
78 Liverpool Road
London, N1 0QD
Tel: 020 7288 9810
Fax: 020 7288 9815
E-mail: editor@itchymedia.co.uk
Web: www.itchycity.co.uk

□□□□□□□□□□□□

Welcome to Itchy 2007

You lucky thing, you. Whether you've bought, borrowed, begged or pinched it off your best mate's bookshelf, you've managed to get your mucky paddles on an Itchy guide. And what a guide it is. If you're a regular reader, you're probably already impressing your friends with your dazzling knowledge of where to head for a rip-roaring time. If, on the other hand, you're a trembling Itchy virgin, then get ready to live life as you've never lived it before. We've spent the last year scouring Edinburgh for the very best places to booze, cruise, schmooze, snooze and lose ourselves to the forces of pleasure. As ever, we've made the necessary, erm, sacrifices in the name of our research – dancing nights away, shopping 'til we flop and of course, eating and drinking more than we ever thought possible. But we're still alive, and now we're ready to do the whole lot again. Come with us if you're up for it – the first round's on us...

KEY TO SYMBOLS

🕐 **Opening times**

🍴 **Itchy's favourite dish**

🍷 **Cost of a bottle of house wine**

💷 **Admission price**

Welcome to Edinburgh

Where most cities will scare you off with their loud noises, unfriendly locals and hefty price tags, Edinburgh will hold you to its bosom, stroke your hair, take your shoes off for you and bring you a nice cup of tea with a biscuit. But it won't stop there.

Once you've finished your cuppa, it'll also give you a full manicure, get you a snazzy new haircut and then take you out for a night of drunken debauchery. Kindly grandma one minute, club raver the next, Auld Reekie is like your best friend, mother and grandma all rolled into one. But not in a weird way, obviously.

If you crave culture beyond compare, the open space of the countryside (ok, and arctic weather) but want it all in one place, then Edinburgh is completely unsurpassed. You can stroll for hours through parks, smell flowers in the Botanic Gardens (who are we to judge?), amble around Arthur's Seat, and then have a drink at a proper country pub, even though you're only minutes away from the buzz of Princes Street.

Alternatively, you could do a spot of shopping, hit some fashionable bars, eat at some of the best restaurants in the UK, or go around all the museums, galleries and historical sites, pointing at paintings and making like you know something about them.

And then there's what happens here in the summer. Come August, Edinburgh is home to quite possibly the greatest festival on earth. You get the best in music, film, dance, and theatre, but it's the Fringe Festival that the world comes to town for, attracted by the cream of comedians and most famous celebrities from around the globe. If you bump into Richard E. Grant, Sean Connery, Max from *Neighbours* or someone from *The OC*, don't be surprised. If you're over 70 or hate anything that's even a little bit creative, don't fret, because the Military Tattoo gives you the chance to watch soldiers playing at being, well soldiers.

But it's not only in summer that Scotland's capital proves itself as a fun-centre. In winter there's an ice rink, a big wheel, and a German market along Princes Street, selling everything from mulled wine to incense sticks, not to mention what happens at Hogmanay. Simply put, we reckon that if Edinburgh were a person, everyone would want to be it. Or be with it. Or be its best mate. Whatever, it'd be top dog.

Introduction

Two hours in Edinburgh

So you've only got a couple of hours in this fair city, and you want to feel like you've 'done' Edinburgh, right? It's a big ask, but if you don't just want to get pissed in a pub all day, then there are other options.

If your inner tourist needs a quick fix, take a wander to Edinburgh Castle, and from there walk down the Royal Mile, taking in all its Scottish glory. If you fancy more exercise, go for a stroll around (or up) Arthur's Seat. Then, have a well earned drink at The Sheep Heid Inn in Duddingston (43–45 The Causeway, 0131 656 6591).

If you're in need of a heavy culture hit, you could go to The Royal Museum (Chambers Street, 0131 247 4422) and from there mosey on down to The National Gallery of Scotland (The Mound, 0131 624 6200) for a squizz at the canvases. You'll be feeling parched by now, so stop off for a drink at the Fruitmarket Gallery (45 Market Street, 0131 225 2383).

If you need something solid to go with your thirst-slaker, then you could try Cargo (129 Fountainbridge, 0131 659 7880), Assembly (41 Lothian Street, 0131 220 4288) or Biblos (1 Chambers Street, 0131 226 7177), which all generously serve both food and drink. If you head to Golf Tavern (30 Wrights Houses, 0131 221 5221), you could even fit in a bit of pitch and putt on their reasonably-sized (and free) golf course. Just hire the clubs and the balls and you're off.

If your plan is to spend 120 minutes shopping 'til you drop, then your best bet is to head down Princes Street. If you want something a little classier, then head down George Street just behind it, where you'll find all the exclusive and expensive shops. Hugo Boss, Jo Malone, Gant and the like all hide out here. And there you have it. Two hours of walking/culture/drinking/eating/shopping-fuelled fun.

Two days in Edinburgh

SLEEP – Let's face it, it all depends on how minted you are. If you're reading from the back seat of a Bentley, you'll be wanting The Balmoral (1 Princes Street, 0131 556 2414), surely the classiest hotel in Edinburgh. The Best Western Hotel (187 Clermiston Road, 0131 535 9988) is a nice but slightly less expensive option, while Brodies Backpacker Hostel (12 High Street, 0131 556 6770) is a sensible choice for those on a shoestring.

EAT – For a wallet-destroying but amazingly good feed, try the Balmoral's Number One (1 Princes Street, 0131 557 6727) or The Witchery (352 Castlehill, 0131 225 5613). For good seafood you'll like Mussell Inn (61–65 Rose Street, 0131 225 5979). If you're a meat fiend then try the amazing burgers at Wannaburger (217 High Street, 0131 225 8770). Or if you shun meat completely in favour of vegetable loveliness, then David Bann (56–58 St Mary's Street, 0131 556 5888) is a firm favourite with veggie types.

SHOP – You'd best try Edinburgh's Harrods equivalent in the form of Jenners (47–49 Princes Street, 0131 225 2841) for all your clothing, smelly stuff, beauty products and Scottish things in general. For cheap DVDs, books and CDs, go to Fopp (55 Cockburn Street, 0131 220 0133). Finally, Royal Mile Whiskies (379 High Street, 0131 225 3383) has souvenirs that also get you pissed.

DRINK – Early riser? You can get a round in at 6am in Penny Black (17 West Register Street, 0131 556 1106). Those who are used to starting a bit later should head to Cargo (129 Fountainbridge, 0131 659 7880) or Montpeliers (159–161 Bruntsfield Place, 0131 229 3115). If you're drinking in New Town try the Jekyll and Hyde (112 Hanover Street, 0131 225 2022).

DANCE – For sordid clubbing and a guaranteed pull, the infamous Lava Ignite (3 West Tollcross, 0131 228 3252) is the obvious port of call. The Liquid Room (9c Victoria Street, 0131 225 2564) is possibly Edinburgh's best club and does a nice line in live gigs too. For something more underground, Cabaret Voltaire (36 Blair Street, 0131 220 6176) offers up slightly more alternative treats for the discerning dancer.

ATTRACTIONS – Let's face it, if you come to Edinburgh and you don't visit the castle, you'll get laughed at. Climbing up Arthur's Seat is also a must, and it's not as hard as you might think. For the rest, just take your pick of any one of the city's massive selection of theatres, museums, galleries and cinemas.

Eat

Eat

CAFÉS

Black Medicine Coffee Co.

2 Nicolson Street

(0131) 622 7209

The mystical feel to the name extends to include the cavernous interior, the rustic furnishings and the beaded, bearded and be-dreaded bar staff. There's an impressive selection of herbal brews and fruit shakes, and there are plenty of good old-fashioned carbs on offer too, with healthy paninis, muffins and biscuits for those who care more about the quality of taste than their size of waist. A great alternative to the capitalist evils of Starbucks for bohos and businessmen alike.

🕑 *Mon–Sat, 8am–6pm; Sun, 10am–6pm*

🍴 *Chorizo, salami and sweet chilli chutney panini, £3.95*

Chocolate Soup

2 Hunter Square

(0131) 225 7669

This is surely the closest one can get to Willy Wonka's famous establishment and there's certainly enough confectionary here to turn you into an Augustus Gloop. There are puritanical alternatives, including bowls of hot porridge and a range of fresh coffees, but only hardened chocoholics should attempt their ultimate challenge: the large Belgian white chocolate soup option, with whipped cream and a chocolate sauce topping complete with an Aero chunk and fudge flake garnish. Even if it kills you, let's face it, it's a good way to go.

🕑 *Mon–Sun, 8am–7pm*

🍴 *Hot chocolate sundae, £2.40*

Elephants & Bagels

37 Marshall Street

(0131) 668 4404

Baps, sir? Or barm cakes, rolls, stotties, butties or buns? Avoid arguments about regional terms for sarnies by plumping for a bagel. Plain of name, but not of nature, especially not when they're freshly baked here, or at sister spot The Elephant House on George IV Bridge (which also does hot dishes in the evenings). Despite their worryingly gynecological-sounding name, Itchy recommends the delicious 'Shmear' flavoured cream cheese toppings, with a steamed milk almond 'Moo'. Boring breadstuffs can foccacia off.

🕑 *Mon–Fri, 8.30am–6pm;*

Sat–Sun, 9.30am–5pm

🍴 *Bagel with smoked salmon, £3.15*

Favorit

19–20 Teviot Place

(0131) 220 6880

This place is designed with the greedy in mind: mounds of chilli-nachos, steaming bowls of pasta, or platters of tapas might be followed by stacks of syrup-covered waffles, ice-cream sundaes or a Ben and Jerry's coke float. A diner in the truest sense (all chrome and red leather), Favorit prides itself on delivering whatever you want, whenever you want. Well, within reason obviously. They won't deliver an Indian elephant to your front door at 5am, for example. With last orders taken into the early hours, reasonable menu-based wishes will be granted.

🕒 *Mon–Sun, 8.30am–2.30am*

🍽 *Favorit nachos with jalapeno chillis, £3.95*

💷 *£11.25*

Kalpna's

2–3 St Patrick's Square

(0131) 667 9890

If, like Withnail, you 'want something's flesh,' then Kalpna's probably isn't for you. But even Itchy the insatiable carnivore (there's a cartoon in that somewhere) was amazed at how good the food was. With various awards for being generally amazing at doing Indian vegetarian food, Kalpna's serves delicious curries which are so good you won't even miss the meat. Plus you might be able to get into those jeans again. At lunch they do an excellent all-you-can-eat buffet for £6 as well. No doubt you'll be trying to bhaji to the front of the queue.

🕒 *Mon–Sat, 12pm–2pm & 5.30pm–10.30pm*

🍽 *All you can eat lunch, £6*

💷 *£10*

Plaisir Du Chocolat

251–253 Canongate

(0131) 556 9524

Ok, so you might say, 'Come on, it's just chocolate,' but that would be like saying Jessica Alba is 'just a woman.' Selling the best chocolatey things to be found anywhere, ever, from truffles and individual chocolates to chocolate cakes and an amazing 53% cocoa hot chocolate (which is what we'd ask for if we were only ever allowed to drink one thing for the rest of our lives). It may be a bit pricey, and there's a distinct danger of wanting to be sick due to chocolate and cake overload, but simply put, if you like chocolate, you'd be mental to miss it.

🕒 *Mon–Sun, 10am–6pm*

💷 *Chocolat chaud, £2.75*

Eat

RESTAURANTS

Beanscene

99 Nicolson Street

(0131) 667 5697

This is where all the cool coffee beans hang out. And if you ask nicely, some people will grind them, put them in a cup and mix them with hot water for you. They'll also serve you tasty food. You could try vainly fighting for the comfy sofas, but they're almost always occupied. There'll also probably be some students sitting around with pages of notes out, trying to prove that they can sit in a café and actually do some work. Which it turns out they can't. Oh, and check the wallet before you go in. It can be pretty pricey.

◉ *Mon–Sat, 7.30am–10pm; Sun, 10am–10pm*

❶ *Cheeseboard, £3.25*

Blonde

75 St Leonards Street

(0131) 668 2917

If hearing the name makes you think 'dappy' or 'naff highlights' then think again. Blonde's classy enough to recommend to your friends, but not so expensive that only the disgustingly rich can afford it. With a cosy atmosphere, a well thought-out menu and some excellent seasonal dishes on offer, it's a student fave, but will appeal to anyone who appreciates their food. Equally able to impress a date or just to provide a great location for a meal out, Blonde is a safe bet for the indecisive or the clueless.

◉ *Mon, 6pm–10pm; Tue–Sun,*
12pm–2.30pm & 6pm–10pm

❶ *Rib-eye steak, £10.95*

◼ *£8.90*

Buffalo Grill

12–14 Chapel Street

(0131) 667 7427

Lusting for a hunk of grilled beef? We thought so. Wild West décor and wafts of Aberdeen Angus beckon diners through the doors of Buffalo Grill. The wood-panelled dining room is the perfect place to ponder which juicy steak or massive burger to order. Prawns or homemade salsa as a starter will keep you busy whilst you're deciding. Keep an eye on the specials board; you might be there for a gem like red wine and mushroom drenched rib-eye. There's no wine list, but with just 75p corkage, you can spring for a bottle of Bordeaux.

◉ *Mon–Fri, 12pm–2pm & 6pm–10.30pm;*
Sat, 6pm–10.30pm; Sun, 5pm–10.15pm

❶ *Roquefort rib-eye, £12.95*

Café Royal Circle Bar

19 West Register Street

(0131) 556 1884

Itchy isn't wont to use the words 'best pub lunch in Edinburgh' lightly, but Café Royal has the best pub lunch in Edinburgh. Perhaps it's because it shares a kitchen with the restaurant at Café Royal, a restaurant so awesome it was featured in the film *Chariots of Fire*. The bar menu isn't enormous, but every dish is comfort food of the best kind. If you don't mind being surrounded by fifty-something men most of the time, the food here is well worth the reward. And the best thing is, they're open for dinner, too.

🕐 *Mon–Sat, 11am–10pm; Sun, 12.30pm–10pm*

🍴 *Lamb and basil burger, £7.95*

💰 *£9.95*

Centraal

32 West Nicolson Street

(0131) 667 7355

So, you want a pint, sofa, and an aquarium? Head to Centraal. Small, sleek, if kinda pricey, this basement hangout is great for dinner and evening drinks. If you like beer you'll have to ponder before ordering – there's an extensive range of the lovely stuff behind this bijoux bar. The food's great, and the Thai green chicken curry will make you an especially happy person. Minus points are awarded for the huge and deeply irritating televisions blaring out terrible pop videos. And there really is an aquarium, which is actually a little weird. That curry makes up for it though.

🕐 *Mon–Sat, 11am–10pm; Sun, 12.30pm–10pm*

🍴 *Thai green chicken curry, £7.50*

💰 *£11.50*

Calistoga

93 St Leonard's Street

(0131) 668 4207

The great thing about California is that Arnie's in charge – perhaps at some point soon his political career'll go the way of his acting one, run out of ideas and spur lots of rehashes of the same old policy ideas. Still, while this restaurant's Californian, it has no resemblance to Arnie's political career, as re-hashes definitely ain't on the menu. Forget burgers and think tasty, healthy, inventive food. The owner is always on-hand to answer any questions as many times as you want, too. Call him over, and he'll be back.

🕐 *Mon & Thu–Sun, 12.30pm–2.30pm & 5pm–10pm; Tue–Wed, 5pm–10pm*

🍴 *Duck leg with South Beach mash, £14*

💰 *£11*

Coconut Grove

3 Lochrin Terrace

(0131) 229 1569

Every so often you want to feel like you're not living in what seems like the coldest place on earth. So sure, a holiday would be great, but if you just need a quick fix, try Coconut Grove. The food is outstanding – not to mention dirt cheap – and if you like your Mexican cooking to be slightly more exotic than a packet of Old El Paso spice mix, which, let's face it is about as Mexican as a kilt, then there's nowhere better. Just prepare to be disappointed after the meal when you step outside and lose the feeling in your limbs.

🕐 *Mon–Sun, 11am–2pm & 5.30pm–11pm*

🍴 *Tequila prawns with rice and salad, £9*

💰 *BYO, corkage, £2*

Eat

Coyaba

113 Buccleuch Street

(0131) 662 9111

Not many people can say they've tried Jamaican and Rastafarian cuisine, but they bloody well ought to. Coyaba caters for a gastronomic niche that's pretty small (hence it being the only Jamaican restaurant in Scotland), but by Jah it's good. By no means a cheap restaurant, it's still barrels of fun with lively staff, constant reggae music, and of course gallons of rum. Just try to resist asking them to pass the duchie 'pon the left hand side. For some reaon they didn't find this as funny as we did.

🕐 *Tue–Thu, 6pm–10pm; Fri–Sat, 6pm–11pm; Sun, 6pm–10pm*

🍴 *Traditional curry goat, £13.50*

💷 *£10.50*

First Coast

99–101 Dalry Road

(0131) 313 4404

So it's not in the swanky middle part of town, and you may have to brave the odd strange glance and insult from a tramp or two to get there, but First Coast is well worth the walk. With plenty of dishes to choose from, and catering for veggies, shameless carnivores and fishy types, it'll keep everyone happy. Add to that a fancy interior, a good wine list, plus a jam roly poly dessert so tasty you'll never settle for a Jammy Dodger again, and you've got yourself an excellent dinner venue.

🕐 *Mon–Sat, 12pm–2pm & 5pm–11pm*

🍴 *Honey roast ham with sauerkraut and mustard sauce, £10.95*

💷 *£9.95*

David Bann Vegetarian Restaurant & Bar

56–58 St Mary's Street

(0131) 556 5888

Oozing with Scandinavian chic, this veggie hotspot is not your average hippie/communist tofu joint. The dishes are excitingly complex and the bold flavours and hearty portions will pleasantly surprise even the most robust Angus-fed Highlanders. The rich but not too filling hummus is a great starter, and should leave you room for the creamy risotto or a stuffed Portobello mushroom. Mains tend to be a tad pricey considering the lack of meat, but what did you expect from a bunch of trendy hippies?

🕐 *Mon–Sun, 11am–late*

🍴 *Risotto verde, £9.75*

💷 *£10.80*

Hadrian's
Balmoral Hotel, 1 Princes Street
(0131) 557 5000

Younger sibling to the Michelin-starred Number One, Hadrian's brasserie has picked up quite a few tricks from its big brother, sporting a menu influenced by the latter's award-winning chefs. The food blurs the line between traditional Scottish and no-holds-barred modern cuisine, haggis is wrapped up in a wonton, Scottish salmon is served up with Mediterranean couscous and sun-dried tomato vinaigrette. Save a few quid with the dinner menu of the month, which gives you three courses plus a cocktail for £20.95.

🕙 *Mon–Sat, 12pm–2.30pm & 6.30pm–10.30pm; Sun, 12.30pm–3pm & 6.30pm–10.30pm*
🍴 *Gressingham duck spring roll, £15.50*
💷 *£17*

Henderson's of Edinburgh
94 Hanover Street
(0131) 225 2131

This is where to come if you're dining with vegetarian or vegan pals, especially if you're after a light lunch. Although mainly frequented by Green Party-voting, middle class professionals with babies and elderly relatives, it offers a break from the student populace. The food is just the right side of natural and rustic although the interior does feel like a canteen. Who knew you could have a dozen different types of salad? This place proves that eating healthily doesn't have to mean cardboard and a lettuce leaf. Or the stick of Satan that is celery.

🕙 *Mon–Sat, 11.30am–3pm & 4.30pm–10pm*
🍴 *2 course lunch offer, £8.95*
💷 *£12.95*

Hector's
47–49 Deanhaugh Street
(0131) 343 1735

Ok, so the poor sod got his arse kicked by Achilles, but he was still pretty hard. And Achilles was all but invincible, so it was a bit unfair. Anyway, no doubt he'd be proud of this place if he were still around/ever existed. Intimate and complete with candlelight ambience, Hector's is pretty special. An excellent lunch, dinner and brunch menu, fresh juices, and Sunday papers for when those pre-evening conversations are just too much like hard work, it's thought of everything. Except being called Achilles.

🕙 *Sun–Wed, 12pm–12am; Thu–Sat, 12pm–1am*
🍴 *Cooked breakfast, £6*
💷 *£9.50*

Howies
10–14 Victoria Street
(0131) 225 1721

Howies is one of those rare places where you can eat top quality food without having to resort to selling members of your family on eBay to afford it (well, we say 'members of your family' – we mean 'grandma'). Whether a two course lunch at £9.95, or a three course dinner at £19.95, you can eat impeccable food without having a heart attack when the bill arrives. Add to that small, intimate surroundings, a comprehensive wine list and a celebrated banoffee pie, and you've got yourself a top class eatery.

🕙 *Mon–Sun, 12pm–2.30pm & 6pm–10.30pm*
🍴 *Cajun battered king prawns starter and chicken breast with mozzarella main, £17.50*
💷 *£10.95*

Eat

Izzi

119 Lothian Road

(0131) 466 9888

Now it's all well and good hearing the cool kids talk about their sushi and sashimi diets, but we've all had an off-putting, pungent whiff of the slimy stuff at some point. Izzi should be enough to change your mind – with not so much as a whisper of the word franchise in earshot, this is probably the closest you'll get to an oriental gastronomic orgasm. Though their Chinese menu isn't much cop and the prices seem a little steep, it matters little. Once you've tasted the sashimi you'll be hooked on the stuff from now on, Izzi-peasy.

🕒 *Mon–Sat, 12pm–11.30pm;*
Sun, 12.30pm–11.30pm

🍴 *Sirloin steak teppanyaki, £13*

💰 *£12.50*

Jacques

8 Gillespie Place

(0131) 229 6080

Ok, so they may have left us in the lurch for a war or two, and sure they can be about as friendly to foreigners as Jesus would be to Judas at a reunion dinner, but the French aren't all bad. Just look at their food. Wholesome and flavoursome, it's no wonder the French sneer at our kebabs and chips. For the mussel lovers, try the ones in bacon and brie: they're, well, brie-liant. And as for the ambience, it's about as cosy as a snug bug in a rug. With a water bottle. You get the idea.

🕒 *Mon–Sat, 12pm–2.30pm & 5.30pm–10pm;*
Sun, 11am–5.30pm

🍴 *Pre-theatre two course meal, £11.90*

💰 *£9.95*

Kismot

29 St Leonard's Street

(0131) 667 0123

An unfortunate location means that this family-run restaurant misses out on the customers that flock to the other popular Indian restaurants in the area. But the delicious food is well worth trying to find it. Service is top-notch, partly due to it being pretty quiet, but perhaps also because this is the only Indian restaurant we know where the waiters wear kilts. Any spice lovers out there with something to prove (or who simply have teflon mouths) should go for the ultra-spicy Garram Massalam – it'll blow your mind. Or at least your taste buds.

🕒 *Mon–Sun, 4.30pm–11.30pm*

💰 *BYO*

Mariachi

7 Victoria Street
(0131) 623 0077

Picture a Mexican restaurant in your mind. Now put that restaurant on the cobblestone corkscrew that is Victoria Street. Everything about Mariachi is exactly as you'd expect: red and green décor, a menu featuring nachos, tacos, chicken and steak, and a few sombreros scattered about the restaurant. The food is as you'd expect as well – it ain't going to set the world alight, but nonetheless, it's a good solid Mexican. The frozen margaritas are delicious, and this is perhaps the only restaurant in the city that does them, so grab a pitcher, some nachos and enjoy.

🕐 *Mon-Sat, 12pm-11pm; Sun, 2pm-11pm*
🍴 *Arroz con pescado, £8.95*
💰 *£10.95*

The Mussel Inn

61–65 Rose Street
(0131) 225 5979

If you were expecting a tavern staffed by fishermen you'll be sorely disappointed, but seafood lovers need look no further. The menu may look a bit bare: it's mussels, scallops, or oysters here, but with styles ranging from Scottish to pan-Asian there are enough options to tickle anyone's fancy. The seafood is as fresh as a breeze up the kilt, so go for a light sauce rather than taste-killing breading. If it's that you're after, grab a box of frozen fish fingers. However, for the bi-valve inclined, this is the place to be.

🕐 *Mon-Thu, 12pm-3pm & 6pm-10pm;*
Fri-Sat, 12pm-10pm; Sun, 12.30pm-10pm
🍴 *Skewered king scallops, £15.50*
💰 *£12.30*

The Mosque

50 Potterow
(0131) 667 1777

Through an inconspicuous archway on West Nicolson, a bevy of cooks are standing over huge vats of curry and rice, providing lunches to the impoverished students of Edinburgh. Well, to the ones that don't own castles. Open seven days a week, and with meals for well under a fiver, The Mosque Kitchen has become something of a culinary institution. If you can cope with paper plates, plastic cutlery, and all-season al-fresco dining you'll be treated to huge portions and the chance to sample some inimitable 'Mecca Cola'. It'll also be (an albeit tiny) kick in the balls for those corporate folk at Coca-Cola. Hooray.

🍴 *Vegetable or meat curry and rice, £3.00*

Native State

32–34 Potterow
(0131) 662 9788

Full of the obnoxious type of students by day, and full of student societies getting leathered by night, Native State is not for the faint hearted. Or anyone with taste buds. Or eardrums. Or the desire to have a nice time. Cavernous, dingy and full of uncomfortable furniture, Native State effortlessly combines aesthetic hell with bad service and rubbish food. Luckily, there are many, many great eateries within spitting distance of this tasteless hole. Which makes it all the more surprising that Native State is always inexplicably packed. Why, people?

🕐 *Mon-Sun, 9am-1am*
🍴 *Burger, £5.75*
💰 *£9.95*

Eat

Negociants

45–47 Lothian Street

(0131) 225 6313

So close to the university it could double as an exam hall, Negociants is always full of students. Hardly surprising; it's quirky and warm with good tunes, and the hot chocolate is mighty fine. Bleaker in the evenings, Negociants is best for cosy lunches and morning coffees, and the menu carries a good selection of fresh soups and salads, and panini-type contraptions that will set you up for an afternoon lectures/ data input. The bill shouldn't upset you too much either. Go, and have the nachos.

🕐 Mon–Thu, 12pm–10pm; Fri–Sat, 11am–2.30am; Sun, 11am–10pm

🍴 Nachos as mains, £6

💷 £10.50

North Bridge

20 North Bridge

(0131) 556 5565

If you ever need to impress someone, be it girlfriend, mother-in-law or parole officer, look no further than the two-storied marble and oak dining room at North Bridge. Be sure to book a table on the mezzanine so you can leer at the peasants below who forgot to call ahead. Despite the posh interior, the food here is reasonably priced and dreadfully delicious. Be sure to have a pre- or post-dinner drink at the stainless steel and glass bar while you remind yourself how cool you are for not eating at the Pizza Hut next door.

🕐 Mon–Sun, 12.15pm–2.30pm & 6pm–10.30pm

🍴 Tuna steak and mash, £14

💷 £13.50

Fried and tested

So you forgot to stop drinking endless lines of shots, and now you're paying for it. Life can be so cruel. But all's not lost, it's just a case of finding the right breakfast cure. For the best fry-ups go to **Toast** (146 Marchmont Road, 0131 446 9873), which serves everything from scrambled eggs and salmon to cakes, smoothies and fresh juices. **Hector's** (47–49 Deanhaugh Street, 0131 343 1735), does much the same job, only in a different place. To replace all those lost fluids and whatnot, try **Juiced Up** (100 Bruntsfield Place, 0131 558 1199), which even has a smoothie tailored for the poor hungover fools that go there. Pick one of these bad boys and you'll be feeling better in no time. It's just getting there that's the problem...

Oloroso

33 Castle Street
(0131) 226 7614

Despite being one of the best restaurants in Edinburgh, hardly anyone's even heard of Oloroso. Thanks to some near-Masonic secrecy, you're only gonna find it if someone tells you about it. So now you know. Sure it's a bit pricey, but it boasts spectacular views of Edinburgh, it serves amazingly good food, and if you tell people about it they'll think you're in some sort of secret society or something. Oh, and they might think you're classy as well. So long as they don't realise you got the tip off us. Don't worry, Itchy won't tell.

🕓 *Mon–Sun, 12pm–2.30pm & 7pm–10.30pm*
🍴 *Highland beef, prices vary*
💷 *£14.50*

The Outsider

15 George IV Bridge
(0131) 226 3131

Intimate, private and stylish. Unfortunately it's also dingy. You can just about see your plate if, while eating, you tilt your head and stop obstructing the spotlights. A shame, as they clearly put lots of thought into presentation. The service is attentive until you've finished your main course, at which point the darkness makes you invisible to waitresses. Despite this, the food is delicious and sharing is encouraged. Therefore, take a date, the gloom will hide your physical defects and the décor will be proof of your sense of style.

🕓 *Mon–Sun, 12pm–11pm*
🍴 *Confit Gressingham duck with warm chorizo, £9.70*
💷 *£12.10*

Original Khushi's

9 Victoria Street
(0131) 220 0057

Please don't be put off by the gaudy interior, the new premises are a little glitzy, but the food is still great value for money and very tasty. It looks a bit more like a nightclub than a good old curry house, but it's still very popular with everyone, so booking's advisable, especially at the weekends. It's lost some of its relaxed atmosphere since moving, but the newfound swankiness doesn't stop the grub being amazing. Nowhere else can you feel like a curry will lead to a cabaret show without leaving your seat. For curry in a hurry, try the lunch menu.

🕓 *Mon–Sun, 12pm–12am*
🍴 *Chicken sag, £8.95*
💷 *BYO, no corkage*

Peckham's Underground

155–159 Bruntsfield Place
(0131) 229 7054

How bad can a basement under a delicatessen (minus any natural light) really be? Pretty bad, obviously, but luckily this is an exception. Food is average, making it better than half of the tripe garnishing Edinburgh's streets and the fact that hot drinks are available in a size known as 'Ridiculous' is always amusing. Add to that an extremely cosy atmosphere, forever-friendly service, and seasonal menus, and you've got a very well-kept secret hidden in the depths of posh Bruntsfield. Not for claustrophobics, mind.

🕓 *Mon–Sun, 10am–12am (last orders, Mon–Fri, 10pm & Sat–Sun, 10.30pm)*
🍴 *Thai green curry, £6.75*
💷 *£9*

Eat

Stac Polly

8–10 Grindlay Street & 29–33 Dublin Street

(0131) 556 2231

The idea of ground up animal bits inside a sheep's stomach may not sound that appetising, but you'd be surprised. Whether you want to try haggis, neeps and tatties, or just stick with the steak or venison, Stac Polly provides the best in modern Scottish cuisine using lovely local ingredients. With a firm emphasis on classy but informal, Stac Polly impresses without intimidating. There's two Stac Pollys in Edinburgh, each with a completely unique menu. As Scottish as a kilt but not as cold.

☺ *Mon–Fri, 12pm–2.30pm & 6pm–11pm; Sat–Sun, 6pm–11pm*

🍴 *Roast loin of venison, £18.95*

💲 *£14.95*

The Stand

5 York Place

(0131) 558 7272

www.thestand.co.uk

Nothing's done by ha ha-lves at this comedy club; get belly laughs and belly fillers too. It won't be cold twisty fries or a school jumper-grey burger you're hilariously spraying all over the crowd either. They do great value meals (like their famous slow-cooked chilli) made from scratch, with the brilliant punchline that on weekday lunchtimes chow and a show is just £5. More guffaws than when Itchy ran out of fingers and ended up in A&E with a Hula Hoop stuck somewhere we shouldn't have threaded it.

☺ *Full menu, Thu–Sat eve, Sun lunch; 'Out to Lunch' £5 deal, Mon–Fri, 1pm–2pm*

🍴 *See website from 10am for daily food deal*

Toast

146 Marchmont Road

(0131) 446 9873

Names can be misleading. Take Toast for example. Sure you can buy toast if you want, but given the food on offer that would be a pretty foolish choice, with cooked breakfasts, croissants, salmon, scrambled eggs and homemade cakes on the menu. We'd say it was like an orgasm happening in your mouth, if that didn't mean something completely disgusting. Add to that the fact that the brunch menu is available until 3pm, and you've just made a new best friend. Make sure Toast is on your Christmas card list.

☺ *Mon, 10am–5pm; Tue–Sun, 10am–10.30pm*

🍴 *Full breakfast, £5.75*

💲 *£12.50*

The Tower

Museum of Scotland, Chambers Street

(0131) 225 3003

Sounds kind of mystical doesn't it? Like a fairytale or something. Well eating at The Tower might remain a fantasy to some forever and ever, as most of us would have to sell organs on the black market to be able to afford it. Having said that, for those that can, The Tower provides not only excellent food and service, but breathtaking views of Edinburgh. If you're lucky enough to visit on a sunny day, (you won't be), then you might even get to sit outside. It's also on top of the Museum of Scotland, so you could maybe fit a quick bit of culture in as well.

☺ *Mon–Sun, 12pm–11pm*

🍴 *Moroccan spiced lamb, £20*

💲 *£13.75*

The Villager
49–50 George IV Bridge
(0131) 226 2781

Cool and stylish, Villager's stencil-lined walls and comfy sofas create a funky and laid-back atmosphere; however, you will still have to claw your way through shiny professionals and students with cash to get to the best tables. The menu is pretty extensive though, and crammed with global-themed dishes, the best of which is probably the vodka-martini mussels. The staff are also shiny and super-friendly, although they will insist on bringing you huge jugs of water stuffed with cucumber. And one can have too much cucumber-flavoured water.

🕒 *Mon–Sun, 12pm–9.30pm*
🍴 *Vodka-martini mussels, £6.25*
🍷 *£11.50*

Vittoria
113 Brunswick Street
(0131) 556 6171

Vittoria is one of the long-standing members of the Edinburgh restaurant scene. It's been around for 60 years, but it's still looking respectable in its old age. The atmosphere is warm, and the décor is distinctly Italian. The menu is so extensive that you'll get hungry just trawling through all the choices, with everything on offer from traditional dishes like pizza and risotto, through to sausage, bacon, egg and chips. Oh, and be careful with the dessert. If you opt for the cheesecake, prepare to suppress the moans of ecstasy, or they might just throw you out.

🕒 *Mon–Sun, 10am–late*
🍴 *Cheesecake, £4.95*
🍷 *Glass, £3.50*

The Witchery
352 Castlehill, Royal Mile
(0131) 225 5613

Well-known by everyone with a bit of cash to splash around, and probably the most famous restaurant in Edinburgh. It's also the favourite port of call with all the superstars. Matt Groening, Michael Douglas, Jack Nicholson and Pierce Brosnan have all eaten here, to name just a few. If you still need a bit of arm twisting to part with your dineros, the coven-baked food's absolutely spellbinding (they're broom-sticklers for perfection), and the setting is beautiful and completely unique. Dannii Minogue called it the 'perfect lust den'. We say it's the wickedest witch in Scotland.

🕒 *Mon–Sun, 12pm–4pm & 5pm–11.30pm*
🍴 *Roast fillet of Buccleuch beef, £29.95*
🍷 *£13.75*

Test of moral fibre

ALRIGHT, SO WE'RE ALL SUPPOSED TO BE EATING ETHICALLY NOWADAYS. BUT WHAT WE WANT TO KNOW IS WHETHER ANY OF THE MONKEYS THAT BANG ON ABOUT THIS STUFF HAVE EVER TRIED IT OUT WHEN PICKING UP SOME POST-PUB STOMACH FILLERS. IT'S A BLOODY NIGHTMARE. OBSERVE:

Illustration by Si Clark, www.si-clark.co.uk

1 Food miles – According to some environmental fascist or other, it's not ecologically friendly to eat stuff that's been flown across the world when you could chomp on courgettes grown much closer to home. Not according to our friendly burger van, however.

Itchy: 'Excuse me, but how many food miles has that quarter pounder done?'

Burger man: 'What?'

Itchy: 'How many miles has it travelled to end up here?'

Burger man: 'Ten miles, mate. Straight from Lidl to this spot.'

Itchy: 'But what about where it came from originally? What about the sourcing?'

Burger man: 'Saucing? I've got ketchup and mustard, you cheeky sod. And it's free, not like him down the road and his "10p-a-sachet" bollocks, now you gonna buy this burger or what?'

'Reckon you could catch enough fish for all the UK's chippies using a fishing rod?'

2 Sustainability – It's not meant to be the done thing to eat fish caught in a way that stops our scaly friends reproducing fast enough to prevent their numbers dropping. Sadly, no-one's told our local chippy.

Itchy: 'Is your cod line-caught?'

Chippy owner: 'Yeah, it's caught mate. How else do you reckon it comes from the sea?'

Itchy: 'No, I'm asking if it was caught using a fishing rod.'

Chippy owner: 'You reckon you could catch enough fish for all the UK's chippies using a fishing rod?'

Itchy: 'Erm, no...'

Chippy owner: 'Right, well there's your answer then.'

Itchy: '...but, you know that you should only really eat fish from sustainable sources don't you?'

Chippy owner: 'Oh yeah? According to who? The media? Reckon all that coke they're on's organic? Produced locally, is it?'

Itchy: 'Well, it's not always possible to consume entirely ethically...'

Chippy owner: 'My point exactly. One cod and chips then is it?'

WHO
WHAT
WHERE
WHEN

IS X

LUXARDO X TEAM COMING TO HOT NIGHTSPOTS NEAR YOU!

GAMES, GIVEAWAYS, COMPETITIONS, PRIZES

WWW.LUXARDOXTEAM.CO.UK FOR MORE ABOUT WHO, WHAT, WHERE & WHEN X IS

LUXARDO
1 8 2 1
SAMBUCA

THE MARK OF SUPERIORITY

Drink

Drink

BARS

Amicus Apple

17 Frederick Street
(0131) 226 6055

Fancy a cocktail with Guinness, vodka, and a description as cryptic as *The Times* crossword? Maybe lounging on a plush leather divan alongside a mural by Bernie Reid – the guy responsible for the chic Dragonfly décor – and munching on pan-fried scallops as you eagerly await the start of Club Trashicana? If so, you'll find Amicus a most amenable partner to the drink-fuelled catharsis that is a Friday night.

◉ *Mon–Sun, 11am–12am;*
Food, 11am–9pm
🍴 *Rib-eye steak, £15.50*
💷 *£11.95*

Bar Kohl

54 George IV Bridge
(0131) 225 6936

If one drizzly night spent sitting in a car park listening to sad radio phone-ins and getting drunk on a bottle of Glenn's ('the exciting vodka') has put you off the tough stuff for life, then you might not be Russian over to Bar Kohl. There are over 250 different vodkas, as well as 54 flavoured Finlandia fillies for you to break in, from Mississippi mud pie to milkshake flavour. Of course, you could be a wimp, sit in a dark corner and just have some of the on-tap lagers. But we say respond to the Kohl of the wild; you're sure to end up having a Stoli good night.

◉ *Mon–Sat, 4.30pm–1am*
💷 *£11*

The Basement

10a–12a Broughton Street
(0131) 557 0097

Slap bang in the middle of the city, but without the stinging slap to the wallet of the ludicrously expensive George Street, The Basement is one of the coolest places in town to drink in. Forget drippy, dingy and whingey; think bright, colourful, vibrant and stylish. The music policy is funky and upbeat, the staff are friendly though verging on lunacy (they wear ker-azy, Base-mental Hawaiian shirts to confirm the point), and the food is top-notch. Get down.

◉ *Mon–Sun, 12pm–1am;*
Food, Mon–Sun, 12pm–10.30pm
🍴 *Rump and merlot pie with*
cheese and onion mash, £6.95
💷 *£8.50*

Bennet's Bar

8 Leven Street

(0131) 229 5143

For a proper pint in a proper pub, get thee to Bennet's. An Edinburgh institution, this bar has a huge range of ales and whiskies to whisk you away to a land full of intricately carved wood and stunning high ceilings, populated by a kooky mix of locals, students, scribblers, musicians and thesps. Situated close to a clutch of art-house cinemas and theatres, it's a great post-performance retreat. The world maps on the tables may have inspired many a cross-continental adventure, but this near-perfect pub is as good a reason as any to stay at home.

Mon–Sun, 11am–12am; Food,
Mon–Sun, 12pm–3pm & 5pm–8pm

Candy Bar

113–115 George Street

(0131) 225 9179

Thought human cloning was a long way off? Take a look inside Candy Bar. They're all good-looking, but you can barely tell them apart: all dollies, no mixtures. This super-cool venue originated in Glasgow, and has spread its model-seeking tentacles to Edinburgh. If you can avoid feelings of... well, inadequacy, then the excellent cocktails make it a great place to get candy caned, and there's some pretty good food as well. Plus hanging around with gorgeous people may get you a sympathy shag.

Mon–Sun, 11am–1am;
Food, Mon–Sun, 12pm–9pm
Thai chicken noodles, £6.75
£14.75

Borough

72–80 Causewayside

(0131) 668 2255

Cool, understated and elegant, this Causewayside bar is worth the trek. A chilled atmosphere is topped with comfy sofas and finished with a twist of zesty soundtrack; the perfect partner to their cucumber martini – surely the most erotic, exotic use of this vegetable, bar none. Heathens should appreciate the wide range of draught beers too, and everyone will love the Scottish mussel and crab claw platter. There's no 'rough' in this Borough.

Mon–Sun, 7.30am–1am;
Food, Mon–Thu, 12pm–10pm;
Fri–Sat, 12pm–11pm
Scottish mussels and crab claws, £9.25
£13.45

Cargo

129 Fountainbridge, Edinburgh Quay

(0131) 659 7880

Foo'canal, what are all them pink, blue and green lights twinkling at the end of this here waterway? That'll be Cargo, me laddie, a cool, low-key bar with private booths as well as outdoor seating for the brave/foolish. Plasma screen televisions with pretty moving patterns on them will entertain you there if the company doesn't, and there's cocktails and grub for all. Plus, the Co-op funeral parlour's just over the towpath – handy for those who like to overindulge themselves.

Mon–Sun, 11.30am–1am;
Food, 12pm–10pm
Cargo grilled cheeseburger, £8.95
£11.95

Drink

Cloisters

26 Brougham Street
(0131) 221 9997

If you're worried that God will smite you down for drinking in a church, fear not. It's been thoroughly deconsecrated by an authorised deconsecrator, so getting drunk in here is now perfectly acceptable. It's not a very big pub, but it's great if you can get your arse on a seat, as they have a mahoosive selection of real ales on tap. It also caters for whisky lovers, though it's not the kind of place you should head to if you're a sucker for the alcopops. It stops serving food early though, so you might have to go elsewhere if you're into your soul food later in the evening.

⚫ *Sun–Thu, 12pm–12am; Fri–Sat, 12pm–12.30am; Food, Mon–Sun, 12pm–3pm*

Dragonfly

52 West Port
(0131) 228 4543

Dragonfly is a cocktail bar. Dragonfly is not a West End bow-tie haven for pretence. People who go to the 'Fly love it for what it is. With lively bar staff, crazy tiger statues (one of which was recently thieved, leading Dragonfly to offer a reward for its safe return home) and random decorations that seem to get more interesting with every drink, this bar's not just a place for a social soirée. It's somewhere that you could call home – if it weren't for the fact that they kick you out come 1am. Give their Mai Tai a blast if you fancy getting blasted.

⚫ *Sun–Thu, 5pm–12am;*
Fri–Sat, 4pm–1am
❷ *£10.50*

The Crags

58 Dalkeith Road
(0131) 667 4518

If you've ever met, talked to, accidentally looked at or breathed the same air as a student at Edinburgh University, then no doubt you'll be familiar with The Crags. It's a bit out of town, but it's right next to Pollock Halls, where all the first years live. It's a Scream pub, so of course it looks like someone vomited it into existence; it's bright, garish yellow is enough to hurt your brain on a hungover morning. Having said that, if you own a Yellow Card, you can help yourself to cheap drinks and food during selected times. Maybe it is worth braving the blinding décor.

⚫ *Mon–Sat, 12pm–1am; Sun, 12.30pm–1am; Food, Mon–Sun, 12.30pm–7.30pm*

Halo

3 Melville Place
(0131) 539 8500

Owned by Keith Murray, the son of steel and football magnate David Murray, Halo is as close to vogue as a bar can get. You'll be surrounded by mirrors, tiny pin-prick-lights and smooth leather interiors. You'll be eating luscious tapas, drinking inspired cocktails and surprisingly not being smacked for asking the bartender for a 'slow, comfortable screw against the wall'. Smooth tunes flow through a buzzing, yet au fait, crowd, as bottles of Bud are swigged alongside Manhattans. Halo doesn't try to be the last word in cool, it just is.

⚫ *Mon–Fri, 11am–1am; Sat, 4pm–1am; Food, Mon–Fri, 11am–10pm; Sat, 4pm–10pm*
❷ *£11.95*

Drink

Harvey Nichols Fourth Floor Bar

30–34 St Andrew Square
(0131) 524 8350

Ok, so it's in Harvey Nichols, it's frequented by Edinburgh's social butterflies and it's expensive. But don't let this put you off, because despite Harvey Nics' upmarket, fashionable reputation, the Fourth Floor Bar is surprisingly relaxed. Great rooftop views and attentive service make it a perfect venue for late-night drinks and the cocktail list throws up some pretty innovative offerings. The drinks may be a bit pricey, but if you feel short-changed, you can always load up on free bar snacks.

Ⓒ Mon, 10am–6pm; Tue–Sat, 10am–12am; Sun, 11am–6pm

Ⓐ £13.50

Indigo Yard

7 Charlotte Lane
(0131) 220 5603

You'll probably have to trample over several hapless victims to get to the bar, but you may just find it's all worth the wait. Alternatively, you may find that the yuppie types comparing their well-ironed banknotes are all a bit tedious. If you can just rise above all the nonsense about 'cutting deals' then it's possible you'll actually have a good time. With minimalist wooden furnishings, Indigo Yard is your consummate trendy bar – and the food isn't bad value either.

Ⓒ Mon–Sun, 8.30am–1am;
Food, Mon–Sun, 9am–10pm

Ⓘ Sweet chilli beef noodles, £7.50

Ⓐ £14.50

Iglu

2b Jamaica Street
(0131) 476 5333

Remember when there'd be a new, really talented kid at school and everyone loved him, leaving you feeling all inadequate? Well, that new kid is Iglu. Not only have they come along and claimed a hatful of prizes for their food and chefs, but they're winning over the locals as well. And rightly so. It really is enough to make other bars weep. Everything's organic, and there are DJs and live acts performing throughout the week. Even KT Tunstall has played there. It's enough to make you sick.

Ⓒ Mon–Thu, 4pm–1am; Fri–Sun,
12pm–1am; Food, Mon–Thu,
6pm–1am; Fri–Sun, 12pm–1am

Ⓘ Organic lamb chops, £14.95

Drink

The Last Drop

74 Grassmarket

(0131) 225 4851

Cheerily, The Last Drop's name has nothing to do with drinking, but the fact that the last public hanging in Scotland took place on the square outside. So there's a factoid to impress your mates with. A dingy but charming pub, The Last Drop has cosy booths for couples and vampires alike. It's also located on the Grassmarket, which is crammed with pubs and restaurants, all vying for your money. A good stop-off before a night of clubbing, or just a good bet for when it inevitably starts pissing it down in the middle of the day. Hard to bag yourself a seat sometimes, mind.

Ⓒ *Mon–Sun, 11am–1am;*
Food, Mon–Sun, 11am–7pm

The Merlin

168–172 Morningside Road

(0131) 447 4329

To be honest, being a wizard and all, Merlin could probably have created a slightly better bar than this one. Having said that, it's still pretty good. But as it's in Morningside (where uppity folks like JK Rowling live), it's not exactly for the thrifty. With some leather sofas for those who aren't too fond of moving, and some pool tables for those who aren't too fond of sitting, it's a good hang-out for the few cool student-types who hang Morningside-way.

Ⓒ *Mon–Wed, 11am–12am; Thu–Sat, 11am–1am; Sun, 12.30pm–12am; Food, Mon–Sat, 12pm–10pm; Sun, 12.30pm–10pm*
Ⓘ *Duck wraps with hoisin sauce, £4.75*
Ⓟ *£9.55*

Montpeliers of Bruntsfield

159–161 Bruntsfield Place

(0131) 229 3115

We like to call it 'one size fits all' because we're not really sure whether it's a bar, a restaurant or just a generally cool place to hang out of an evening. But then again, we don't really care exactly what it is. Excellent food, a great atmosphere, and a huge drinks selection make it an excellent choice of venue for dates, family meals, parties or pre-club drinks. So basically, head on over anytime, and Montpeliers will serve you well. Oh, but get there early. Those seats sure get taken fast.

Ⓒ *Mon–Sun, 9am–1am; Food, 9am–10pm*
Ⓘ *Grilled salmon with sugar snap pea risotto, £6.95*
Ⓟ *£12.95*

NB's

1 Princes Street
(0131) 556 2414

The slogan for this watering hole is 'Princes Street's Number One Bar'. This is a horrible pun on its address, and whoever thought of it should be tarred and feathered. However, of all the gin joints on Edinburgh's main drag, this is certainly one of the best. The sumptuous leather sofas engulf the patrons, while the relaxing music and dim lighting make this a welcome respite from the hustle and bustle of New Town. Just don't wear trainers and you'll avoid the embarrassment of politely being asked to leave the premises.

Mon–Thu, 11am–11pm; Fri–Sat, 11am–1am; Sun, 12pm–11pm
£15

Opal Lounge

51 George Street
(0131) 226 2275

This is where Justin Timberlake, Pink and that lot ended up after the MTV Europe awards were held in Edinburgh. And it's kind of easy to see why. It's pretty swanky, there's an award-winning cocktail maker in their ranks, and it's open 'til 3am, seven days a week. Plus it serves an array of Asian-orientated food. Sounds perfect, doesn't it? Well not exactly. It's damned expensive, and there'll be a lot of posh students and pretentious wannabes in the crowd. Definitely not a place to go for a cheap pint.

Mon–Sun, 12pm–3am; Food, Sun–Fri, 5pm–10pm; Sat, 12pm–10pm
Duck spring rolls with hoi sin, £4.10
£13.95

The Office

21 Lothian Road
(0131) 228 3404

A lot less cringe-worthy than the television program of the same name, The Office is a cool hangout for the slightly wealthier members of this fair city. A pint of fruit beer is tasty, but you may cough it up through your nose once you see the bill, which they'll bring to your table for no extra cost. But the food's decent, so it's good for a much-needed pint and meal after another mind-numbing day at the office. We know, we even make ourselves chuckle sometimes.

Mon–Thu, 12pm–12am; Fri–Sat, 12pm–1am; Sun, 12.30pm–12am; Food, Mon–Sun, 12pm–9pm
Nachos supremos grande, £6.95
£11.25

Oz Bar

33 Candlemaker Row
(0131) 226 7190

For those of you who can't get enough of a good theme bar, you'll find the surf shack inspired bar, AC/DC soundtrack and cold bottles of Victoria Bitter to be a good old slice of the outback in grey, cobbled Old Town. However, having visited, it seems that there are only about four people in Edinburgh with this interest, as that's the average number of drinkers here during the day. Be sure to make your visit before a weekend night if you want to avoid spending your whole evening playing eye tango with the surly chav across the bar from you.

Mon–Sun, 1pm–1am
£10.80

Drink

The Pear Tree

38 West Nicolson Street

(0131) 667 7533

Lurking in the shadows of Edinburgh's ugliest building, Appleton Tower, The Pear Tree is a favourite haunt of Edinburgh University students, and is accordingly packed with them. Housed in a building dating back to 1749, The Peartree has plenty of old-world charm with its oak-panelled walls and dim lighting. Happily, this doesn't extend to the clientele; the booze-fiends here provide a vibrant atmosphere. In the summer, and even in the winter, the massive beer garden is a great place to enjoy a pint of real ale away from the crowded interior.

Mon–Thu, 11am–12am; Fri–Sat, 11am–1am; Sun, 12.30pm–12am

Ryan's Bar

2 Hope Street

(0131) 226 6669

When delving into the depths of Edinburgh's West End, you should also expect to be delving to the bottom of your wallet. As soon as you see that it's three quid for a pint of Tennants, you'll know that if you're out to get scoofed you're in the wrong place. But if you're looking for something a bit upmarket, maybe Ryan's is for you. Slapped right in the middle of one of the city's business districts, Ryan's is a good choice for that swanky lunch or a sneaky mid-tea-break pint.

Sun–Thu, 7.30am–12am; Fri–Sat, 7.30am–1am; Food, 7.30am–10pm

Beer battered haddock, £2.95–£3.25

£10.80

Rick's Bar

55a Frederick Street

(0131) 622 7800

If you want to be all James Bond (Sean Connery rather than Timothy Dalton), then try going for martinis at Rick's. They're damned delicious. And with friendly staff, a great atmosphere and superb cocktails, Rick's pretty much ticks all the boxes for what a classy bar should be. Swish and upbeat, it's equally good for large groups or dates, as there's a darker, more intimate area near the front. It's bound to impress anyone you take there. You smooth thing, you.

Mon–Sun, 7.30am–1am; Food, Mon–Wed, 9.30am–10pm; Thu–Sat, 9.30am–11pm; Sun, 9.30am–10pm

Seared duck breast, £13.45

£13.95

The Southern Bar

22 South Clerk Street

(0131) 667 2288

The Southern used to be grubby, but a facelift has transformed this popular hangout, frequented by both students and Edinburgh folk. There are lots of places to sit, including secluded raised areas for romantic tête-à-têtes and hushed chat. There are also sometimes people with guitars lurking about, but don't be alarmed – this is just an indication of the pub's commitment to hosting live music. Great for relaxed evenings out, and for the aforementioned live entertainment. A small word of warning: take a jumper – it's nice, but it's cold.

Mon–Sun, 11am–1am; Food, Mon–Sun, 12pm–8pm

Drink

The Sportsters Bar

1a Market Street

(0131) 226 9560

It's not lying you know. This really is a bar for sportsters. Or, put another way, people who go to the pub for watching football, and not talking. One minute spent inside its walls will soon reveal why. Forget a huge crowd of drunken Celtic supporters crowded around one projector screen, this one is like a Bond-baddy control room, featuring multiple screens, from projectors to televisions in booths. And you can get almost any game. They have a Playstation 2 and internet access, so there's absolutely no excuse for being even remotely sociable.

🕐 *Mon–Sat, 11am–12am; Sun, 12.30pm–12am; Food, Mon–Sat, 11am–10.30pm; Sun, 12.30pm–10.30pm*

Sygn

15 Charlotte Lane

(0131) 225 6060

The sign outside Sygn is so discrete that it's almost as if they don't want you to find them. Add to that the fact that it's known locally as 'The Bar With No Name' and you start to wonder whether it's on the run from the law or something. But then again, it always seems to be packed, most probably because it's an excellent bar. Apparently their Remy Martin Louis XIII cognac is very reasonably priced too. Just take our word for it. Hopefully this suave bar is a Sygn of things to come. Ahem.

🕐 *Mon–Sun, 10am–1am; Food, Mon–Thu & Sun, 10am–10pm; Fri–Sat, 10am–11pm*

🍴 *Grilled lobster risotto, £16.95*

🍷 *£12.95*

Drink

Tigerlily

125 George Street

(0131) 225 5005

Tigerlily has been carefully crafted with a very exclusive clientele in mind. If you're looking for pumping dance anthems and folk with more flesh showing than you'd get on late-night Channel 4, don't come here. Food is princely and the drinks list is eclecticism gone wild, drawing from every single continent. With cocktails such as the vibrantly sweet 'Chilean Chica' to their tongue-tingling take on a Whisky Sour, this is international boozing. And you never know, you may just pull a millionaire.

🕑 *Mon–Sun, 8am–1am;*

Food, Mon–Sun, 8am–10.30pm

🍴 *Cinnamon duck breast, £12.50*

💲 *£15.50*

Traverse Bar

10 Cambridge Street

(0131) 228 5383

If there's a place to discuss poncy art and theatre, then this is it. Attached to The Traverse Theatre, which is host to plays showcasing new writing talent, it's chock full of luvvies, theatre goers, celebrities and drinkers alike. The bar is so long that it seems to trail endlessly off into the distance, like some sort of long, alcohol-laden yacht, and as a whole the Traverse is generously spacious. The music's reliable, the bar staff always seem jolly enough, and there's a decent selection of drink and food.

🕑 *Mon–Wed, 10.30am–12pm; Thu–Sat, 10.30am–1am; Sun, 5pm–12am*

🍴 *Chicken, avocado and cheese panini, £4.95*

💲 *£10.50*

PUBS

Bad Ass

167 Rose Street

(0131) 225 1546

Perhaps unsurprisingly, this pub is under the same management as Dirty Dicks, and if they're anything like us, they must enjoy tittering at the names. But what's confusing is that Bad Ass is more of a bistro than a pub. Even though it looks like a pub from the outside, the inside is kinda pub-like and they serve beer on tap. Told you it was confusing.

🕒 *Mon–Thu, 11am–12am; Fri–Sat, 11am–1am; Sun, 11.30am–12am; Food, Mon–Sat, 11am–11pm; Sun, 11.30am–11pm*

🍴 *Highlander chicken, £9.75*

💰 *£11.85*

The Blind Poet

32 West Nicolson Street

(0131) 667 0876

Plush sofas, metal surfaces and cool furnishings are all happily missing here. Think tweed jackets with patches on the elbows, old comfy chairs, and worn-out carpets to get more of an idea of what The Blind Poet is all about. Small, intimate and comfortable, with famous posters on the walls, quotes from poets and philosophers kicking around the various blackboards, and beer-stained chairs, it's all about character. And this pub has oodles of it. This is the kind of place where you won't feel like a complete ponce for talking about something vaguely intellectual.

🕒 *Mon–Sun, 11am–1am;*

Food, Mon–Sun, 5pm–10pm

Games for a laugh

Finding a pool table may be easy, but what about some games that are a little bit different? **The ¼ Gill** (77 Clerk Street, 0131 622 7236) has a darts board for the aspiring Phil Taylors among you. Get a few drinks in and work on the darts-player paunch. If you want arguments, try **The Maltings'** (81–85 St. Leonard's Street, 0131 667 5946) large collection of vintage board games, including Monopoly, Scrabble,

and the potentially disastrous Jenga. Remember, it's not the taking part that counts, it's the ritual humiliation of your friends. Alternatively, if you want to try out a quiz machines and get into an argument with your mates about who the world's leading producer of tin is (it's Bolivia), **The Golf Tavern** (30–31 Wrights Houses, 0131 221 5221) and **Biddy Mulligans** (94–96 Grassmarket, 0131 220 1246) will sort you out.

Drink

Brass Monkey

14 Drummond Street

(0131) 556 1961

Shhh... we're going to let you in on a secret. Brass Monkeys' main bar may be pretty cramped, but it has a neat little trick up its sleeve. Go through to the room on the right, and hey presto, it's a room that's all bed. That's right, a whole room that's a bed. As in there's a room, and then there's a huge bed in it. It's like a ménage-à-40. It's not just for show mind, it's also so that you can find a nice comfy place to lounge around on when you're watching films, which they show daily on their projector screen. They play good chill-out music, giving it an atmosphere that's perfect for meeting new people.

🕒 *Mon–Sat, 11am–1am; Sun, 12pm–12am*

Drouthy Neebors

1–2 West Preston Street

(0131) 662 9617

Just around the corner from the Meadows, the recently renovated Drouthy's is always full of students and locals. There is a great selection of beers and spirits, all reasonably priced so you and your mates can afford a few rounds while watching the football on one of the many plasma screens. The seating is on two floors, so beware the staircase if you've had a few too many. It certainly isn't the most interesting pub in Edinburgh, but it's always a great bet for a few pints/glasses of white wine with the a gang of lads/lassies.

🕒 *Mon–Sat, 11am–1am; Sun, 12.30pm–1am; Food, Mon–Sat, 12pm–9pm; Sun, 12.30pm–9pm*

Dirty Dicks

159 Rose Street

(0131) 225 4610

If you're not too disgusted by the name, which is unashamedly gross, then you'll find that Dirty Dicks is actually a decent pub. Plus it's clean too. And there's not a willy in sight unless you choose to hang around in the men's lavatories. With a low-beamed ceiling, candles and lamps, it's a pretty mellow and inviting place. The pub that is, not the toilets. With cask-conditioned ales, homemade soups and hearty pies, Dirty Dicks is a great stop-off, and less packed than your average Wetherspoons.

🕒 *Mon–Thu, 11am–12am; Fri–Sat, 11am–1am; Sun, 12.30pm–12am; Food, Mon–Sat, 11am–11pm; Sun, 11.30am–11pm*

🍴 *Dirty Dick's steak and ale pie, £7.45*

Golf Tavern

30 Wrights Houses

(0131) 221 5221

Although it sounds like it should be populated by doddering old men talking about golf etiquette, Golf Tavern is far from a dingy geezer's pub. Easy to spot at a distance thanks to the flames outside, it shows all the sport, has proper food, and an all-important quiz machine. Its name comes from the fact that it has its own 36 hole pitch-and-putt golf course – possibly the only free golf course in the world. It's probably true because it's a bit pants, but it's still good for a laugh, and you won't get old poshos tutting at your drive. Bonus.

🕒 *Mon–Sun, 10am–1am; Food, Mon–Sun, 10am–10pm*

🍴 *Burger and chips, £5.50*

Jekyll & Hyde

112 Hanover Street

(0131) 225 2022

Named after the book of the same name by Robert Louis Stevenson (oh yeah, we're cultured), Jekyll and Hyde is decorated in the Gothic style (ie, it's dark and has weird scary things hanging on the walls). A great venue for a drink or two with some mates, it's also got one of the most well-hidden toilets of all time. Check out the imitation bookcase on the wall if you're stuck. Yeah, they're in there somewhere. Good luck finding them when you're lashed, which you will be with a few of their excellent cocktails inside you.

🕒 *Mon–Thu, 12pm–12am; Fri–Sat, 12pm–1am; Sun, 12pm–late; Food, Mon–Sat, 12pm–9pm; Sun, 12.30pm–9pm*

The Malt Shovel

11–15 Cockburn Street

(0131) 225 6843

Much like the Green Giant, The Malt Shovel is large, verdant and hard to miss. But whereas the Green Giant might kick your arse or force-feed you sweetcorn, The Malt Shovel will lovingly provide you with a cosy environment in which to enjoy up to 92 whiskies. Not all at once, mind. A pub that attracts pretty much everyone, The Malt Shovel is a favourite with all and sundry; locals, students, office workers and tourists all make it their haunt. Every Wednesday night, local duo Rantum Scantum play, and they seem to be a crowd pleaser.

🕒 *Mon–Wed, 11am–12am; Fri–Sat, 11am–1am; Sun, 12.30pm–11pm; Food, Mon–Sun, 12pm–9pm*

The Links

2–4 Alvanley Terrace

(0131) 229 3834

If you've ever wondered why the streets are empty during football matches, take a quick peak inside The Links. Don't try and get in though, as you'll probably get trampled to death. With pool tables, tasty food, multiple plasma screens and projectors on every wall, it's always packed. Plus it has some nice outdoor seating for those few rain-free days. A great pub if you can avoid it during footy matches, where decent views of a screen, movement and breathing are all heavily restricted.

🕒 *Mon–Sun, 9am–1am;*
Food, Mon–Sun, 9am–10pm

🍴 *6oz sirloin steak, £9.25*

💷 *£9.60*

Drink

The Outhouse

12a Broughton Street Lane

(0131) 557 6668

Down a slightly dodgy-looking alley sits The Outhouse, a not-so-dodgy pub in New Town. Although the drinks are pretty pricey, the beer garden makes up for it. With heaters and regular barbecues, it's warm and it has good grub – what more can you ask for? The inside is small but there's a pleasant atmosphere, even though you may have to cope with those damned backless 'cube' stools. And it can be a bit cold. So bring your own huge sofa and log fire and you'll be set.

🕒 *Mon–Sun, 11am–1am; Food, Mon–Thu, 12pm–6pm; Fri–Sun, 12pm–4pm*

🍴 *Burger and chips, £4.95*

💰 *£10.60*

The Oxford Bar

1a Market Street

(0131) 226 9560

Fans of Ian Rankin novels will recognise this as Inspector Rebus' local, but even if you aren't a mystery addict, you'll still find plenty to enjoy about this pub. No neon bar counters, exotic vodkas or people under the age of 50 here, but for that you get a boozer that's brimming with authenticity. Rest assured though, this isn't an old man's pub with three patrons who shoot you the evil eye if you're not a regular. Friendly chat abounds, there's a great selection of ales and plenty of old wooden chairs to settle into, if you can squeeze through the mob huddled around the bar.

🕒 *Mon–Sat, 11am–1am; Sun, 12.30pm–1am*

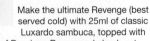

Penny Black

17 West Register Street

(0131) 556 1106

Only the most hardened drinkers have ever experienced the phenomenon that is the opening of Penny Black. Not because it's hard to find or because you have to get tickets or anything, but because it opens at 6am, which means that it's open a whole hour before *The Big Breakfast* used to be on. Seriously, they really open that early. And that means that you'll find serious drinkers getting a round in here. From thirsty construction workers to post-club drinkers, posties to alcoholics, lorry drivers to weirdos, visiting Penny Black is a sure-fire sign that you're cool. Or in need of a new liver. One of the two.

☻ *Mon–Sun, 6am–12am*

The Shakespeare

65 Lothian Road

(0131) 228 8400

Ok, so you had to study endless plays by the bastard when you were at school, but it's time to forgive and forget. He's a lot less threatening when he's a pub. Showing all the football matches, and providing a good local drinker in the middle of the city, Shakespeare is finally serving a use. Attracting a mixed crowd, it has a quiz night every week and karaoke for those who enjoy humiliating themselves. Just remember though, your rendition of Bonnie Tyler's *Total Eclipse of the Heart* is not as good as you think.

☻ *Mon–Tue, 11am–12am; Wed–Sat, 11am–1am; Sun, 12.30pm–11pm; Food, Mon–Sat, 12pm–8.30pm; Sun, 12.30pm–8.30pm*

Décor blimey

Pub décor – boring, eh? Fear not, with us you can drink in style. For an aquarium, shiny chrome surfaces and comfortable sofas, try **Centraal** (32 West Nicholson Street, 0131 667 7355) which will delight, relax and confuse your senses in equal measure. For an experience just as bewildering, try **The Forest Café** (3 Bristo Place, 0131 220 4538), a haven for arty/hippy types that's kind of like a drinky place and an art gallery all in one. There's also **Lulu** (125b George Street, 0131 225 5005), which has lanterns on the bar and décor that's somewhere in between oriental-inspired and the bar in *A Clockwork Orange*. Roses, glass and red dominates. There's a dance floor that's lit up from below with sound-responsive disco lighting. Hardly innovative, we know, but it's a beautiful piece of kit if we ever saw one.

Drink

The Sheep Heid Inn

43–45 The Causeway, Duddingston Village

(0131) 656 6951

More medieval than the Black Death, Scotland's oldest pub has hung around all these years for good reason. The Sheep Heid Inn is a truly Scottish pub, and a very fine one at that. Dating from around 1360, it can count Mary Queen of Scots and King James VI among its previous visitors. It has good beer, decent food, a car park and a skittle alley. Yes, that's right. A skittle alley. Forget the Megabowl, this is the place to hit the lanes. A perennial favourite on sunny days. Oh, and try their barbecued venison burgers. Brilliant.

◉ *Mon–Thu, 11am–11pm, Fri–Sat, 11am–11.30pm; Sun, 11am–11pm; Food, Mon–Sun, 12pm–8pm*

The Steamie

72–74 Newington Road

(0131) 667 9019

Combining the old-fashioned pub look with chrome and the like sounds like a recipe for disaster, but somehow The Steamie just, well, works. Like haggis, the horrendous ingredients somehow combine to make something that'll keep you coming back for more. With a glass front for the voyeur in you, as well as a dark cavernous area at the back for the misanthropes, The Steamie caters for most tastes. There's excellent graffiti art inside, and it's not a bad place just to sit and have a pint either. There are also some smart cocktail deals and pool tables upstairs as well.

◉ *Mon–Sun, 12.30pm–1am; Food, 12.30pm–6pm*

Standing Order

62–66 George Street

(0131) 225 4460

It's big, it's spacious, it's cheap, and it has absolutely zero character. Effortlessly combining bland décor with an atmosphere which is reminiscent of purgatory, coming to this Wetherspoons pub is a bit like having an accident and ending up in a very horrible and embarrasing situation. Like tripping up and lying face-down in a puddle of your own piss, for example. You wait ages for a table, make a mad rush for it like you actually want to stay, and then wonder why the hell you ever bothered once you sit down. Utterly and totally forgettable. Meh.

◉ *Mon–Sat, 9am–1am; Sun, 10am–1am; Food, Mon–Sun, 10am–10pm*

The Three Sisters

139 Cowgate

(0131) 622 6801

The Three Sisters is one of those Marmite pubs. Either you'll love it for the fact that it's full of students, hen nights, TV screens and people in fancy dress about to go on a night out, or, you'll hate it for the exact same reasons. True, it's a nightmare getting in sometimes, thanks to only one entrance which scores of people of all dimensions have to fit through, but some folk find that sort of thing enjoyable. If you don't like huge crowds, try it early on a weekday evening, and see what it's like without half of Edinburgh's population crammed into it.

◉ *Mon–Sat, 9am–1am; Sun, 12.30pm–1am; Food, Mon–Thu & Sun, 12pm–9pm; Fri–Sat, 12pm–8pm*

Stay regular

Illustration by Joly Braime

AIN'T NOTHIN' QUITE LIKE STEPPING INTO A BAR AND BEING GREETED AS ONE OF THEIR OWN. HERE'S ITCHY'S GUIDE TO BECOMING AS REGULAR AS CLOCKWORK SOMEWHERE NEW

1 Learn the name of the publican's partner/pet/mum – Take a couple of mates and stand at the bar within earshot of the publican and engage in the 'what would your porn name be?' game (combine your pet's name with your mum's maiden name). After a while, get the publican to join in, and make up some new variants designed to extract info about the names of spouses, dad, etc. Next time you walk in, you'll be able to greet them with a friendly, 'Alright Dave, how's Sandra doing?'

2 Have your own pint mug – Take a vessel and ask them to keep it behind the bar for you. Then whenever you walk in, you can sup your beverage in style. You may want to save this for the second visit.

3 Know the pool rules – If they've already got a set of rules in place, learn what they are, loiter near the table and make sure you pounce upon any infraction to loudly proclaim 'That's not how we do things in here'. If there are no house rules, even better – make some up, don't tell anyone what they are, and then soon everyone'll need to ask you before playing.

4 Start a cribbage team – Unless the pub in question's populated by incontinent octogenarians, there's no chance that they'll have one. Get a 'Captain' T-shirt, and swan round asking randoms if they're ready for the big match. They'll have no idea what you're talking about, allowing you to explain your importance to the pub community.

5 Take a dog – Everyone loves a dog. Well, except asthmatics. But who cares about them? Those guys are already having enough of a wheeze.

THE**LIQUID**ROOM

EDINBURGH'S FINEST LIVE MUSIC
VENUE AND NIGHTCLUB

FROM **INDIE** TO HIP HOP,
FUNKY HOUSE TO **ROCK**...

The Liquidroom is open 5 nights
a week from Wednesday to
Sunday 10.30pm – 3am

For gigs, clubs and all live
music events log onto
www.liquidroom.com

THE**LIQUID**ROOM 9c Victoria Street, Edinburgh
T| 0131 225 2564 www.liquidroom.com

LARGE COVERED & HEATED SMOKING GARDEN AT THE REAR OF THE BUILDING NOW OPEN!

Dance

Dance

CLUBS

The Bongo Club
Moray House, 37 Holyrood Road
(0131) 558 7604

Walk past The Bongo Club during daylight hours, and you'll find a quirky little café with exhibitions and all-important rehearsal space. Come night-time, it's still quirky, but it's also blasting out music so loud it'll shatter your eardrums. The Bongo Club has drum 'n' bass, DJs, punk, disco, garage, electro, samba, salsa, jazz, funk, soul, Afro-Latin – well, everything basically. There's also a chilled out café upstairs in case everything gets a little too much for you. So sit down, put your feet up, and relax.

- *Mon–Sun, 8pm–3am*
- *From £3*

City Nightclub
1a Market Street
(0131) 226 9560

The first thing you'll notice about City Nightclub is its size, as it easily holds up to 1,500 people. If you go to the toilet, good luck finding any of your mates again. City is home to some of Edinburgh's most beautiful people, so there's plenty of eye candy around for men and women. It's also got some of the top DJs around, with the likes of 2 Many DJs performing there, as well as DJ Filthee and Tokyo Blu. The Sportsters Bar is next door as well, and is perfect for a bit of football on TV/ Playstation 2/internet access beforehand. They really have thought of everything.

- *Mon–Sun, 11pm–3am*
- *From £3*

Cabaret Voltaire
36 Blair Street
(0131) 220 6176

No space in your moby for Cabaret Voltaire's number? Delete your mum's. Located on quiet Blair Street, this place is the only excuse for going there, but hot-diggedy-damn is it an excellent one. The twin subterranean cavern rooms have free license to be as loud as they want, and they make full use of that allowance seven days a week with headline live gigs and nights more blinding than the sun, where even straitjacket-style dancers end up reaching for the stars. Don't miss Leeds export event Sugarbeat, which has featured sets from Soulwax, Zinc, Yoda, and the mindblowing ASkillz.

- *Mon–Sun, 10.30pm–3am*
- *Prices vary*

Ego
14 Picardy Place
(0131) 478 7434

With a name like Ego, you'd think it might have a bit of attitude, but it feels a lot friendlier than your average club. It's gay-friendly, student-friendly, straight-friendly, you name it-friendly. Drinks go down as low as £1, and admission can be as little as £2, so Ego is even wallet-friendly. And with a fish tank in the club, it seems that Ego is also friendly towards little fishies. There are a couple of dance floors for clubbers, with r 'n' b alternating with shamelessly cheesy tunes. This is clubbing with music that's easy to dance to, and made easier to dance to thanks to the cheap alcohol.

- *Sun–Thu, 11pm–3am*
- *From £2*

Lava Ignite

3 West Tollcross

(0131) 228 3252

Ok, so it smells slightly of sick when you walk in, and from thereon in the smell gets worse, but Lava Ignite is a potentially fun night out. It's huge and always packed – there are five bar areas, three large rooms, and all the space is pretty much dancefloor. There are always good deals on cocktails, beers and mixers to take advantage of, and the music caters for everyone from the r 'n' b kru to people who want to hear cheesy old 70s tunes. Admittedly this is a venue best-enjoyed if you're drunk, but Itchy still reckons it's a fine place to let your hair down.

ⓒ *Wed & Fri–Sun, 10pm–3am*

ⓐ *From £2*

The Liquid Room

9c Victoria Street

(0131) 225 2564

If this place was any more of a complete leg-end, it would grow toenails, while its roster of epic DJs must make paltrier clubs feel about two (verucca-covered) feet tall. Whether you want big live acts – Long Blondes, Black Keys, The Levellers, Lee 'Scratch' Perry, Willy Mason – or faultless record spinning spanning alt to urban, you're Li-quids in. Wednesdays' indie DJ actually plays the requests he promises, and you won't grow a beard in the time it takes to get served. Itchy's pick is Thursdays' Snatch Social: kooky comedy cabaret, retro porno style and drinks at 50p.

ⓒ *Wed–Sun, 10.30pm–3am*

ⓐ *£1–£5, more for special nights & live gigs*

Dance

Madogs

38a George Street

(0131) 225 3408/225 2600

Madogs is less your full-on nightclub and more your bar with some gigs and a dance floor kinda thing. It's got some reasonably cheap drinks, and it's probably most famous for being the place where Ray Wilson made his name. You know, the guy who replaced Phil Collins in Genesis... right. With friendly service and open seven nights a week, Madogs is good as a place for a few drinks or a big night out. There are DJs to keep you entertained, and you can still hear people well enough to actually have a conversation that's slightly more advanced than, 'Music's loud, isn't it?'.

© *Mon–Sun, 8pm–3am;*

⊕ *Prices vary*

Prive Council

47 Hanover Street

(0131) 225 8808

The drinks at Prive Council are so cheap that you'd be forgiven for thinking they were feeding you battery acid. And you wouldn't be that far off to be honest. Still, with spirits selling for as little as 50p a shot, and drinks before midnight generally costing £1.50, there's little room for complaint. The music is pretty good, but it's small and the dance floor isn't that conducive to cutting shapes. Still, tucked away and hard to find, Prive Council is one to bear in mind, and it tends to be free admission before 12am – a bonus on an already cheap night.

© *Mon–Thu, 10pm–3am; Fri, 4pm–3am; Sat, 9pm–3am*

⊕ *Free before 12am, then prices vary*

Massa

36–39 Market Street

(0131) 226 4224

If the prospect of hearing the *Baywatch* theme played at 2am appeals to you, then you may enjoy Massa. Having said that, enjoying Massa would also entail you liking overcrowded clubs, ridiculously long bar queues and rude bouncers. It's not so much a place you go to have a good time as a place where you go to remind yourself of just how cruel life can be. Popular with the posh students on Wednesday nights, and popular with other people other nights, presumably Massa's doing ok for itself. We're just not really sure why.

© *Wed–Thu & Sun, 10pm–3am; Fri–Sat, 5pm–3am*

⊕ *From £5*

Why Not?

14 George Street

(0131) 624 8633

Invariably receiving the answer, 'Because it's shit', Why Not? is one of Edinburgh's most horrendous clubs. Setting aside the fact that the queue to get in is endless, and that the clientele are so posh they'd turn into pashminas if left alone for five minutes, it's just plain nasty. The bouncers are total bastards, queuing for a drink takes hours, people will barge into you because they think their daddy owns your daddy, and the music is boring and repetitive. We heard a girl got knocked out in here a little while ago when a disco ball fell on her head. We imagine it's like being kissed by an angel.

© *Mon–Sun, 10pm–3am*

⊕ *From £5*

HEN PARTIES

Distinguishing features: Normally perform their all-female pre-mating ritual in a circular dance around sequined receptacles containing grooming apparel. The leader usually wears a letter L and some kind of sexual apparatus on her head.

Survival: For males under 60, camouflage is the best bet. Itchy recommends a bright pink mini-skirt, padded boob tube and red lippy.

HOMO NARCOTICUS

Distinguishing features: This unusual subspecies is mesmerised by repetitive rhythms and flashing lights, and has a peculiar ability to move all limbs and appendages at once in contrary directions, including eyes and ears.

Survival: These malcos are guaranteed to spill your drink on themselves. Put your bev in a bike bottle or go the whole way and throw a sacrificial pint at them before you start dancing.

Safe and sound

Illustration by Thomas Denbigh

THE DANCE-FLOOR IS A SCARY REALM. IF YOU WANT TO MAKE IT OUT ALIVE, YOU'LL NEED SOME INSIDER KNOWLEDGE, SO GRAB PITH HELMET AND GLO-STICKS AND FOLLOW ITCHY ON A DISCO SAFARI

THE LADS

Distinguishing features: Alpha males indulging in competitive play, such as mixing several beverages in the same glass, and then drinking the whole lot as quickly as possible.

Survival: A propensity to punch the air during power ballads can lead to injury among taller adventurers. Itchy suggests you don a helmet and hit the deck if you hear the line 'Oooh baby do you know what that's worth?'.

UNDERAGE DRINKERS

Distinguishing features: Identified by greasy hair, pale skin and vacant eyes, this genus often regurgitate upon themselves, presenting a hazard to bystanders. Females are impervious to cold and wear very little.

Survival: Enlist their natural predators – larger and more primitive hominids called bouncers, who covet the hair of the underage drinkers, being themselves a furless species.

CABARET VOLTAIRE

BREAKING BOUNDARIES IN MUSIC

36 BLAIR STREET, EDINBURGH, EH1 1QR. T: 0131 220 6176

WWW.THECABARETVOLTAIRE.COM

Gay

Gay

BARS

Café Habana
12–18 Greenside Place
(0131) 558 1270

Sitting next door to the Playhouse, Café Habana is extremely popular with both men and women of the gay persuasion. It probably has quite a lot to do with the fact that there's a small balcony overlooking the main bar, so you can pick a potential target before you swoop down to make your move. This is probably Edinburgh's premium gay-friendly bar, and it's popular too, with outside seating even drawing in the more reticent members of Edinburgh's gay scene.

🕓 *Mon–Sat, 12pm–1am; Sun, 12.30pm–1am*
💷 *£10.95*

Planet Out
6 Baxters Place
(0131) 556 5551

Situated at the top of Leith Walk, Planet Out is so popular with the local gay community that you can consider yourself lucky should you be able to actually move once you get inside. This is usually the venue of choice before everyone moves on for dancing at CC Blooms, and the energy of the place is contagious. It's not big, but it is clever: it's got a smart atmosphere, the bar staff are super-friendly, the music is decent and the prices of the drinks mean you won't have to spend the next two weeks eating only plain toast. Which is never a bad thing.

🕓 *Mon–Fri, 4pm–1am; Sat–Sun, 2pm–1am*
💷 *£11.50*

The Claremont Bar

133–135 East Claremont Street
(0131) 556 5662

Not for the prudish, The Claremont is exclusively for the gay men of Edinburgh, and that means that the tone here is as camp as a row of hats. Think nights involving dressing up in kilts, PVC, rubber, leather and the rest. It's shameless and brazen, and it knows it is. When it's not getting patrons to dress up, it's a friendly pub which serves good food and drink at reasonable prices. A local legend among the people that know it, The Claremont Bar is the kind of place where you can see and be seen.

◉ *Mon–Thu, 11am–12am; Fri–Sat, 11am–1am; Sun, 12.30pm–11pm*
◉ *£8*

Twist

26b Dublin Street
(0131) 538 7775

After a huge renovation job, The Newtown Bar turned into Twist, and it's now looking brand spanking new and impressing the pants off everyone that sees it. What was formerly a male-only drinkery is now lesbian-friendly too, so expect a mixed bunch. TVs around the bar play modern pop videos and some old 80s camp classics, and there's space downstairs for people wanting to boogie. Putting just as much of an emphasis on talking as on dancing, Twist has added an energising, erm, twist, to Edinburgh's gay drinking scene.

◉ *Sun–Thu, 12pm–1am; Fri–Sat, 12pm–2am*
◉ *£9.95*

Cabaret venues

If you're up during the Festival, **The Ladyboys of Bangkok** have become a regular staple show for the punters and one of the most talked-about events at the Fringe, and rightly so. Bright colours, bright dancing, bright music, and dirty comedy, all done to perfection. You'll have to keep on telling yourself that they used to be men, because given the way half of them look, it's pretty easy to forget. For a cabaret treat with a distinctly Celtic flavour, make sure you try **Taste of Scotland** (The Stables at Prestonfield, Priestfield Road, 0131 225 7800). For a little under £50 a head, you get dinner, half a bottle of wine, and all sorts of genuine Scottish shindiggery. It runs six nights a week from April to October, but make sure you book ahead.

Gay

CLUBS

CC Blooms
23–24 Greenside Place
(0131) 556 9331

CC Blooms is unique in that it's the only dedicated gay club in Edinburgh. Sadly, that means that if you're looking for gay-friendly fun, you're going to have to opt for CC Blooms every time. They have two slightly disappointing floors of ear-drum shattering dance and camp disco anthems, and the mirrored dance floor downstairs will make you feel slightly ashamed of your moves, but with a good mix of ages in the crowd, you can have a fabulous time if you go for it and let your hair down.
© Mon–Sun, 7.30pm–3am
© Free

CAFÉS

Blue Moon Café
36 Broughton Street
(0131) 557 0911

The Blue Moon Café is the oldest gay haunt in town, and very friendly to boot. It's a guaranteed safe bet for getting the low-down on what's moving and shaking in the gay world, with all the goss on parties, gay nights and other activities. The tamer gay activities, obviously. There's a good menu on offer, and they serve up a pretty extensive selection of veggie bites for all you meat-haters out there. Just don't blame Itchy when you turn anaemic.
© Mon–Fri, 11am–10pm;
Sat–Sun, 10am–10pm
© Veggie burger, £4.50

Sala Café
60 Broughton Street
(0131) 478 7069

Located just next to the Lesbian, Gay and Bisexual Centre, Sala Café isn't pulling any surprise punches. It's all new and spangly since it was done up as well, so Sala is looking particularly tasty nowadays, like a lot of the clients inside. With a distinctly Spanish flavour and feel, Sala provides everything from tapas to more regular dishes, plus some options for the gay veggies of the world. With an ambience which is both relaxed and alluring, this is one of the more accommodating and low-key gay venues around, so maybe leave the leather chaps at home this time.
© Tue–Sun, 11am–10pm
© Tapas from £3.95

SO YOU'RE A FRIEND OF DOROTHY WHO'S FOUND THEMSELVES IN A NEW TOWN, AND IT MIGHT AS WELL BE THE EMERALD CITY, YOU'RE SO CLUELESSLY GREEN. HOW DO YOU TRACK DOWN THE BEST PINK PLACES? LET ITCHY GUIDE YOUR RUBY SHOES WITH SOME PEARLS OF WISDOM...

Even if their tastes aren't quite yours, they can give you the lowdown on the more subtle gay haunts, and you and Toto will be going loco in no time.

Scally or pally? – Various gay fetishes for chav-style fashions can make

Gay abandoned

There's no place like homo – Just because you're out of the closet doesn't necessarily mean that you love the great outdoors; camping it up isn't for everyone. However, the most kitsch, flamboyant venues are generally well advertised and typically the easiest ones to find; their mass appeal means you usually get a fair old proportion of straights in there too, enjoying their recommended weekly allowance of cheese, but you should have no trouble tracking down a few native chatty scenesters.

it hard to tell a friendly bear pit from a threatening lions' den full of scallies, especially if you've only heard rumours that somewhere is a non-hetters' hot spot. Be cautious in places packed with trackies unless you want your Adid-ass kicked.

Get board – Internet message boards have honest, frequently updated tips; magazines like *Diva* and *Gay Times* have links to local forums on their sites. Click your mouse, not your heels, and get ready to go on a bender.

Shop

Shop

SHOPPING CENTRES

Princes Street Mall
Princes Street
(0131) 557 3759

The Princes Street Mall is the sinking ship of the shopping centre world. It seems to be getting emptier all the time, shops are falling over themselves to leave and people now tend to give it a wide berth. As a result, it's best used as a shortcut for going elsewhere. Wondering why it's such a state? Check out the eating area. It's only fractionally less depressing than lunching in a morgue. Frankly, calling it a mall is pretty generous too: you'd be better off trying to find the latest UK chart releases at a Baghdad market stall.

◉ *Mon–Wed & Fri–Sat, 8.30am–6pm; Thu, 8.30am–7pm; Sun, 11am–5pm*

St James Centre
Leith Street
(0131) 557 0050

Ahh... Saint James. The patron saint of big buildings with shops in them. His mum must be very proud of him, considering he started out running a little cornershop. What with the huge range of major national retail outlets and small specialist shops it has, we're pretty impressed too. Forget walking down the whole of Princes Street to do your weekly shop, you may as well just go crazy and buy everything in the same building. It may seem ambitious, but if you pull it off then you'll save shedloads of time, and you'll hardly have broken a sweat. It's almost like this place is a shopping centre or something.

◉ *Mon–Sat, 9am-6pm; Sun, 11am–5pm*

Speak easy

PULL OUT THESE PHRASES AND THE LOCALS'LL LOVE YOU (MAYBE...)

I cannae be arsed – I don't really think I can be bothered.
Ya aw richt, hen?
– How are you keeping? (to a woman).
Yer aff yer heid!
– You're absolutely mad!
Buckfast – happiness.
There's a wee bonnie lass
– There's a small, atttractive lady.

Whit're ye daeing mon?
– What are you up to good sir?
It's proper dreich, ya ken?
– It's really wet, you get my drift?
Ah goat it aff the broo
– I got it from those nice people at the Employment Exchange.
Ah'll stoat yer wallies
– I'll punch your teeth.
Geeza a swatch at yer...
– Let's have a look at your... (usually followed by a reference to female genitalia).

DEPARTMENT STORES

Jenners

47–49 Princes Street

(0131) 225 2841

Jenners is to Edinburgh what Harrods is to London, and until recently it was the oldest independent department store in the world (sadly it's now owned by those corporate fiends at House of Fraser). Thankfully, it still feels unique, boasting a beautiful building and a quirky Scottish feel, plus top labels at slightly less heart-attack-inducing prices than elsewhere. The only place for those of you wanting to buy something typically Scottish for your mum, other than a deep-fried Mars Bar or a can of Irn-Bru.

☻ *Mon, Wed & Fri–Sat, 9am–6pm; Tue, 9.30am–6pm; Thu, 9am–8pm; Sun, 11am–6pm*

UNISEX CLOTHING

Cult

7–9 North Bridge

(0131) 556 5003

If, like Itchy, you're 'down' with your 'homies', then Cult is pretty much the only place to be. With a good selection of clothes for lads and lassies alike, it daddies its competitors hard. It's not the cheapest shop in town, in fact there's just no way on earth that the prices this place charges are borne out of anything other than unbridled greed – we refuse to believe the stuff's worth this much. Still, when you find something that makes you look smokin' it all seems worthwhile. Peace out dudes. Westside.

☻ *Mon–Wed & Fri, 9.30am–6pm; Thu, 10am–7pm; Sun, 12pm–5pm*

MEN'S CLOTHING

Topman

30–31 Princes Street

(0131) 556 6589

Ok, so it won't set your world alight, but you know what to expect. There's the usual variants on the same two stripy jumpers they've been stocking for the last few years plus some averagely-priced trendy bits for your laddish mates to mock. Topman brand director David Shepherd was once reported as saying that the only people who go to Topman for a suit are preparing for either their first court appearance or job interview. What about all the guys who want to be one of Topman's army of identikit fashion victims?

☻ *Mon–Wed & Fri–Sat, 9am–6pm; Thu, 9am–8pm; Sun, 11am–5pm*

Flip of Hollywood

60–62 South Bridge

(0131) 556 4966

If you've been to Cult then you've probably been to Flip. It's perfect for all you indie kids out there with a thing for b-boy culture: there's loads of denim, leather, retro shirts and mildly humorous/plain unfunny T-shirts. Flip and Cult pretty much overlap in terms of content, and what you can't find in one you'll probably find in the other. They're kind of like a crime-fighting duo, each compensating for the other's weaknesses. Except that they don't fight crime. And they don't have any superpowers. And they're shops. These petty, trivial points aside, the analogy works perfectly.

☻ *Mon–Wed, 9.25am–5.30pm; Thu–Sat, 9.25am–6pm*

Shop

WOMEN'S CLOTHING

Arkangel
4 William Street
(0131) 226 4466

Taking the 'you've got to go out of your way to get the good stuff' principle to new extremes, the two ladies who run this shop undertake twice-yearly shopping trips to Paris and London. Unusual but wearable is what they're going for, so basically they're saving you a hell of a lot of effort and putting all the best things they find in one store. They even have a personal service for when you're not sure whether or not a dress makes you look like a beautiful goddess or a swollen marshmallow. What lovely people.

🕐 *Mon–Wed & Fri–Sat, 10am–5.30pm;*
Thu, 10am–6.30pm

SHOES

Office
79a Princes Street
(0131) 220 4296

Noticeably less funny than the TV program of the same name, but a much better bet for finding a good pair of shoes. The guys at Office may be big evil corporate chaps who count their money every night and cackle wildly about how rich they all are, but if independent shops were this good we'd shop there instead. Excellent for men and women, it's pretty much the only place you can guarantee will have that really cool pair of shoes you once spotted and have been looking for ever since.

🕐 *Mon–Wed & Fri, 9am–6pm; Thu, 9am–*
8pm; Sat, 9am–6.30pm; Sun, 11am–5.30pm

H&M
41–43 Princes Street
(0131) 226 0790

Even though H&M caters for men and women, as usual the chaps get the bum deal while the ladies get a massive selection of cheap, fashionable clothing. With a huge range of cosmetics and accessories as well as all the usual clothes items, it's a haven for all the women out there who want to look good on a shoestring budget. It's also a pretty safe bet for picking up a bargain, a word that most women find so attractive they'd actually like to marry it. Luckily they can't, otherwise H&M would've pretty comprehensively screwed over men in two senses.

🕐 *Mon–Wed & Fri–Sat, 9.30am–6pm;*
Thu, 9.30am–8pm; Sun, 11am–6pm

SECONDHAND

Aha Ha Ha
99 Bow Street West
(0131) 220 5252

No, it's not the noise that a serious record collector makes when they spy a rare A-ha album. It's a wacky fancy dress shop. With a huge pair of novelty glasses above the door and a name like Aha Ha Ha, this is hardly the most serious of fancy dress shops. Ideal if you want to get some cheap crap for your mate's birthday so you can force him to go out dressed as a German porn star or a gay pirate. It's also got loads of humorous sex-related items that you can titter about with your mates. Oh, and the front door says 'pull' on it when you have to push it. Harket that.

🕐 *Mon–Sat, 10am–6pm*

WM Armstrong and Son

83 Grassmarket

(0131) 220 5557

To those in the know (ie, us) Armstrong's is the secondhand shop of choice for... well, pretty much everyone. Whether you're looking to go along to a fancy dress party as a Napoleonic soldier, a cowboy or a goat (ok, maybe not a goat), or whether you're just looking for some good secondhand clothes to parade around in, it's all here. Just try not to be one of those tools who can't tell second-hand clothes and fancy dress apart. There's dressing strikingly, and then there's dressing like a fashion abberation. The only downside is that the place smells a bit like an old people's home. Oh well.

🕙 *Mon–Thu, 10am–5.30pm; Fri–Sat, 10am–6pm; Sun, 12pm–6pm*

FOOD

IJ Mellis Cheesemongers

30a Victoria Street & 205 Bruntsfield Place

(0131) 226 6215/447 8889

If the sign on the front doesn't grab your attention, then the overpowering smell of unwashed feet probably will. With huge blocks of all sorts of cheese on sale, this is the best place in Edinburgh for all the curdled milk lovers out there to find what they want. They also have other local and organic produce, from fruit and chutneys to jams and teas, which means you'll never have to settle for plain old beans on toast again. It also makes for a great hiding place if you haven't washed in days.

🕙 *Mon–Sat, 10am–6pm; Sun, 12pm–5pm*

Lupe Pintos

24 Leven Street

(0131) 228 6241

It's always the same, isn't it? You go on holiday, have a nice beer or three, and then come back swearing you'll find an offie that sells it back home. Then within a week you're getting pissed on Carling again. Luckily Lupe Pintos might help jog your memory. With imports from Mexico, Spain, Italy, America, Japan, Thailand, India and other exotic places, it's got all those products you tried when you were on your travels but thought you'd never see again. They also sell Italian pasta sauces that don't have a photo of a smirking Frankie Dettori on the front of them.

🕙 *Mon–Wed & Sat, 10am–6pm; Thu–Fri, 10am–7pm; Sun, 12.30pm–5.30pm*

Shop

BOOKS

Analogue

102 West Bow

(0131) 220 0601

The first port of call for people who want to buy a birthday present that appears thoughtful but took all of five minutes to find, Analogue has all the books that Waterstones doesn't. With illustrated books on graffiti art, interior design, architecture, photography and the like, Analogue throws up some genuinely awesome books. They also sell limited editions of things like bags and posters as well, so you can guarantee that nobody else will have them. It's almost enough to make you feel special.

🕒 *Mon–Sat, 10am–5.30pm*

Armchair Books

72–74 West Port

(0131) 229 5927

Open 'til late at night, Armchair Books deals specifically with vintage and pre-owned books from all genres, with some texts dating back to 1840. Great for finding all those old books you want.

🕒 *Mon–Sun, 10am–10pm*

Blackwell's

53–62 South Bridge

(0131) 622 8222

So much more than just a bookshop. This place has everything you want. If everything you want is books and cards. What can we say? We're easily pleased.

🕒 *Mon, Wed–Fri, 9am–8pm; Tue, 9.30am–8pm; Sat, 9am–6pm; Sun, 12pm–6pm*

Waterstone's

13–14 Princes Street

(0131) 556 3304

You always feel safe in a Waterstone's. In fact, we think there's something about a shop that has more than one floor that just screams 'quality'.

🕒 *Mon–Fri, 9am–8pm; Sat, 9am–7pm; Sun, 10.30am–7pm*

WH Smith

Cameron Toll Shopping Centre

(0131) 672 3777

Is it a bookshop? Is it a newsagents? Is it a sweetshop? It's whatever you want it to be, so grab some wine gums and a Mills & Boon and stop asking questions.

🕒 *Mon–Wed, 8am–6pm; Thu–Fri, 8am–7pm; Sat, 8.30am–6pm; Sun, 10am–5pm*

MUSIC

Avalanche

17 West Nicolson Street

(0131) 668 2374

Nestled worryingly close to Fopp, you'd be forgiven for thinking that Avalanche gets slightly overwhelmed by its local competitor. Luckily, it's excellent for music, obscure B-sides, limited editions and new releases which aren't quite popular enough for HMV to stock. A genuine treasure-trove of CDs which will make you go all nostalgic about bands you'd completely forgotten about. Yet another music store which you will both love and hate for its ability to suck money out of your pockets. For those of you who pay for music, it's a must.

🕐 *Mon–Sat, 9.30am–6pm; Sun, 12pm–6pm*

Ripping Records

91 South Bridge

(0131) 226 7010

When you're competing with Avalanche and Fopp, you need to be doing something pretty monumentally cool just to keep up with them and not feel like the loser in the corner. Luckily Ripping has a cunning little trick up its sleeve. With a comprehensive list of all the gigs going on all over Scotland (ok, so that'll just be Glasgow and Edinburgh then), it not only tells you everything that's going on, it lets you buy all your tickets there as well. So if you're lacking in imagination, willpower or fitness, just sit in Ripping for a day and plan a year's worth of gigs.

🕐 *Mon–Wed & Fri, 9.30am–6pm; Thu, 9.30am–7pm; Sat, 9am–6pm; Sun, 12pm–5.30pm*

Fopp

7–15 Rose Street

(0131) 220 0133

Probably the single most dangerous shop in the world. With all the latest DVD and CD releases, plus a smattering of cult classics, foreign films and an array of cheap and interesting books, it is virtually impossible to enter one of the two Fopp stores and leave without some completely unnecessary, but excellent, purchases. Cue regret weeks later as you rifle through piles of coppers, struggling to afford a ham and mustard sandwich from the local Co-op. Oh well, at least you got two books on Che Guevara and three Hitchcock classics for less than twenty quid. Which are infinitely more enriching than a manky Co-op sarnie anyway.

🕐 *Mon–Sat, 9.30am–7pm; Sun, 11am–6pm*

HMV

129–130 Princes Street

(0131) 225 7008

Hum Music Vocally. That's what we've been led to believe the initials 'HMV' stand for, and we like to obey this instruction to the letter when stood plugged in to the listening posts.

🕐 *Mon–Wed & Fri–Sat, 9am–6pm; Thu, 9am–8pm; Sun, 11am–5.30pm*

Virgin

124 Princes Street

(0131) 220 2230

Don't feel like a corporate whore for shopping here. Some days all you want to do is froth at the mouth in a consumerist frenzy of spend, spend, spend.

🕐 *Mon–Wed & Fri–Sat, 9am–6pm; Thu, 9am–8pm; Sun, 10am–6pm*

Shop

OTHER

All Your Needs

Basement of Flip, 60–62 South Bridge

(0131) 556 2328

If you're into the smoking lifestyle, give in to hemptation and roll up to All Your Needs. It's a basement-based, 24-Camberwell-carat goldmine of papers, grinders, legal highs, shishas and gadgets for those who like to keep their head in the fragrant clouds. Friendly owner Haggis will sort you out with everything you need for your own special 'Burns' nights; pipe up if you want some music (filter) tips too, as he sets the trip-hop decks alight. Surprisingly though, he doesn't like James Blunt.

ⓒ *Mon–Wed, 11am–5.30pm; Thu–Sat, 11am–5.45pm; Sun, 12pm–5pm*

Royal Mile Whiskies

379 High Street, The Royal Mile

(0131) 225 3383

It's pretty much a given that anyone who visits Scotland is going to have to drink Scottish single malt whisky. Whether they do it throwing up all over their new kilt isn't so certain, but there are ways of stacking the odds heavily one way or the other. Anyone keen on puking should head to the nearest cornershop; everyone else should head to Royal Mile Whiskies – one of the most respected whisky retailers around, winning *Whisky Magazine*'s coveted Retailer of the Year award twice in the last five years. They are also keen to point out that all of their staff are whisky enthusiasts. Tremble before their whisky knowledge.

ⓒ *Mon–Sat, 10am–6pm; Sun, 12.30pm–6pm*

Beyond Words Photography

42–44 Cockburn Street

(0131) 226 6636

Don't you just hate it when you try to take one of those epic National Geographic-style photos and just end up completely ballsing it up? You know, that tiny speck on a blurred background with the window reflection that was meant to be a majestic panoramic shot of a camel in the desert, evoking the feel of dust in the nostrils and the spirit of Lawrence of Arabia? Well, these guys seem to have more of an idea what they're doing. They sell all kinds of quality photos, and not a finger on the lens in sight. Their postcards are pretty damned cool as well.

ⓒ *Sun–Mon, 12pm–5pm; Tue–Sat, 10am–6pm*

Gash

www.gash.co.uk

When Itchy's mate Dave discovered this über-classy online erotic emporium, stocking lingerie, cosmetics, books, lotions, and lady-pleasing toys including the 'Tongue Joy', he declared, 'That's just like the rhyming kitchen product; "Gash, loves the jobs you hate"'. This revealed both his dire bedroom prowess and an acute lack of grease-busting knowledge – that's Mr Muscle, not Flash, twazzock. When he's finished with the sink, we've got his girlie some personalised pants to help him patch things up, with a photo of his mug and the words 'Dave, come on down'. Our own deluxe satin pair look stunning, but maybe having them embroidered with 'Itchy' wasn't such a good idea.

IF YOU THINK VEGGIES ARE CRANKY, YOU'LL LOVE THIS. FREEGANS SAY OUR ECONOMIC SYSTEM HURTS THE ENVIRONMENT, TREATS ANIMALS CRUELLY AND WORKERS UNFAIRLY, AND WASTES RESOURCES, SO YOU SHOULDN'T PAY FOR FOOD. IDIOTS. HERE'S HOW WE'D BE FREEGANS…

1. Have a Pret dinner – The bods who run Pret a Manger obviously don't know much about the principles of Freeganism, given how much they throw away each day. Turn up at closing, rummage through their bin bags, and hey presto – free dinner.

2. Kill an animal – Apparently it's legal for you to kill squirrels on your own property. With this in mind, set up a bird table, cover it in superglue and get the pot boiling while you wait for it to become a squirrel lolly. Sure, you might snare the odd bird, but extra protein's always welcome, and the RSPB'll never catch you.

3. Forage – Those in the country could nick apples from trees and scour woodland floors for wild mushrooms. Alternatively, those of us whose parents aren't blood-related to each other could pull half-eaten trays of late-night chips from bins.

4. Mug a milkman – Those bastards don't need all that milk. But you do. Being a freegan isn't conducive to a calcium-rich diet, after all. Wait until your local milky's delivering to a dark area, then knock him out and chug as many bottles as you can before making your getaway.

5. Sniper rifle the zoo – Get up high, and train your gun on the elephant cage. It's not going to be easy to take one of those suckers down with one shot, but if it pays off, you'll be eating like a monarch for weeks. Plus you could sell the tusks on to practitioners of Chinese medicine for extra cash.

Freegan fun

Illustration by Thomas Denbigh

0800700200
FREE
PHONE

G.A.N
SKIP HIRE

AA | driving school

enjoy

**Buy 2 AA driving lessons
and get 1 FREE*.**

Don't miss out! Book your first lesson today.
Call 0800 107 2044.

www.AAdrivingschool.co.uk

AA driving school. Drive your dreams forward

FREE
AA DRIVING LESSON

Your FREE AA driving lesson voucher

Book your first lessons today.
Call 0800 107 2044. Buy 2 lessons, then simply hand this voucher to your
AA driving instructor at your first lesson to arrange your free lesson.

Your Name	**(Instructor use only)** AA Driving Instructor Name
Your Pupil Number	AA Driving Instructor Number

(Given on calling 0800 107 2044)

Code 342 – Itchy

Out & about

Out & about

CINEMAS

Cameo Picturehouse
38 Home Street
(0131) 228 2800

Quite possibly the best cinema you'll visit in this lifetime, with offers so outrageously student-friendly you wonder how they're still in business. After all, how many other places would allow you to watch the latest releases on a Wednesday morning for just a single pound? Oh, and as an added carrot to tempt you there's also a rather cosy little bar inside, so if the film sucks you can always waltz to the foyer and get tipsy enough to make it more tolerable. All of this without so much as a whiff of a multiplex throng. Brilliant.

ⓑ £1–£5.90; Wed, before 12pm, £1

Cineworld
Fountain Park, 130–133 Dundee Street
(08712) 002 000

The Cineworld is comfortably positioned among the other well-known bar and restaurant chains that line Fountain Park, and this is reflected by it being such a popular choice with Edinburgh's cinema-going public. Although it does occasionally screen indie films, this is more often than not the place to kick back in front of the latest blockbuster, with jumbo popcorn in one hand, an overpriced 500g bag of pick 'n' mix in the other and somewhere between two and seven litres of Coke in your lap. It's usually the first choice for drivers too, what with the handy (and refreshingly spacious) car park nestling underneath.

ⓑ £3.70–£6.30

Dominion Cinema

18 Newbattle Terrace
(0131) 447 4771

This little place would probably be a lot more popular if it wasn't hidden away on the fringes of the city centre. If you know anyone who's been there before, then they're almost certain to have gushed about the unparalleled comfort offered by each of the four screens within, one of which includes leather recliners and sofas. Though parking your posterior on these is well worth the price of entry alone, the healthy mix of mainstream and independent films makes it a welcome alternative to the ubiquitous multiplex.

🕑 *Mon–Thu, 3pm–8.45pm; Fri, 12pm–8.45pm; Sat, 11am–8.45pm; Sun, 2pm–8.45pm*

Vue

Omni Centre, Greenside/Ocean Terminal, Ocean Drive
(08712) 240 240

Just to further any social divides that might already be present, the Vue proudly boasts Gold Class screens, offering luxury seating and a fully licensed bar. While wading through the riffraff to reach the screens in the first place is already an achievement, it does take a lot of gall to saunter into said Gold Class screen in front of these gawking eyes. To be honest though, you can get the same cinematic experience in a Scum Class screen without paying a ridiculous price and happily clutching a tub of Baskin Robbins ice-cream instead of a dry martini.

🕑 *Times vary*
💷 *£4.15–£8.95*

Let's get physical

Fancy keeping fit and having fun at the same time? Don't look so sceptical. It's possible, honest. Take **El Barrio** (119 Rose Street, 0131 226 4311), where weekly salsa lessons shatter and entertain in equal measure. Order a Mojito and then try and master complex dance moves without stepping on feet. Failing that, just shed some pounds as you panic at your own incompetence. And if all of that just seems a little bit too classy, then try poledancing. It's fun, nobody gets hurt, you get fit and other people may enjoy watching. Check www.polestars.net for information on classes by experts, or go along to **Western Bar** (157–159 West Port, 0131 229 7983) for inspiration, and then go home and give it a whirl. It definitely beats a run in the freezing cold, and fitness will probably be the last thing on your mind...

Out & about

COMEDY CLUBS

Jongleurs
6–7 Omni Leisure Development, Greenside Place
(08700) 111 960

Hi, we're Jongleurs. You may have heard of us. We're a bit like Wetherspoons but we have slightly less vomit on the walls and we encourage a lot more swearing. Oh, and our drinks are a bit more expensive. But we also offer you comedy which is at the cutting edge of the UK comedy scene, which they don't do, unless your idea of entertainment is watching drunk pensioners fall over. And being the sophisticated chaps that we are, when the comedy's over we're also a club until 3am. Now that's class.

🕑 *Times vary*

The Stand
5 York Place
(0131) 558 7272

We're Adam-Ant; The Stand delivers. Outstanding comedy, top class food, and prices that mean you can afford to go more times than an incontinent pensioner. Really fresh ideas too, like Red Raw on Sundays, showcasing at least eight new funny people for a single quid. Comics tend to be decent quality to the bargain – no lame Butlins-esque cymbal-clash punchlines or jokes so old they've had to travel back in time in their ReTARDIS to fetch them. If you're feeling pissed office at work, try the £5 lunch and show deal; for busting swivel chair blues, it gets a Stand-ing ovation.

🕑 *Mon–Fri, £5 show & meal, 1pm–2pm;*
Mon–Sun, doors 7.30pm

THEATRES

Edinburgh Playhouse Theatre

18–21 Greenside Place

(0131) 524 3333

If you can resist the temptation to say, 'Oh my God, isn't that that guy from so-and-so?' then you'll probably get to see some pretty good stuff at The Playhouse. It may be a firm favourite with D-list celebrities desperately trying to revive their waning careers, but it isn't all bad. So sure, there are reunion tours and a few stage adaptations of musicals that were fairly ropey to start with, but if that doesn't make you want to beat your head to a bloodied lump on the walls, then it might just throw up something kinda entertaining.

💿 *Mon–Sat, 11am–6pm; Sun, from 4pm*

King's Theatre

2 Leven Street

(0131) 529 6000

Have a few drinks and then sit up in the gods of the King's Theatre. Feels like you're gonna fall off doesn't it? But don't worry, you'll probably be fine. It's the price you have to pay for being a cheapskate, but it's worth it. Home to some of the best productions in Edinburgh, including everything from The Royal National Theatre to the slightly more low-brow yearly pantomime, The King's caters for everyone with a vague interest in theatre. It's also allied with the Festival Theatre, so what you can't find at one you can probably find at the other.

💿 *Box office, Mon–Sat, 11am–6pm; Sun, from 4pm*

Festival Theatre

13–29 Nicolson Street

(0131) 529 6000

In a building made almost entirely from glass, The Festival Theatre is more than just a peeping Tom's wet dream. With all of the big productions passing through here at some stage, it puts on some of the more impressive shows that Edinburgh has to offer. Ballets, operas, musicals, dance and drama are all catered for, so you can feel terribly intelligent and sophisticated watching something you don't really understand. Itchy reckons it's a safe bet to claim that it's 'ironic'. Just try not to titter at the guys in tights, particularly if they start to get a bit excited.

💿 *Box office, Mon–Sat, 11am–6pm; Sun, from 4pm*

Royal Lyceum Theatre

30b Grindlay Street

(0131) 248 4848

The crew of the Lyceum have quite a lot in common with the good folk at the Grolsch brewery. Err, no, we don't mean that they always smell of beer. We're talking about the fact that they don't like to rush into things. When they pick a production it sticks around for a while. They savour it, give it a month or so to really grow and be thoroughly enjoyed, and then only let it back into the wild when it's good and ready. This means that even the slow among you will be able to get tickets to something without fear of it selling out, rather than getting trampled in the stampede for tickets at the Kings and Festival Theatres.

💿 *Box office, Mon–Sat, 10am–6pm*

Out & about

Traverse Theatre
10 Cambridge Street
(0131) 228 1404

The plays at The Traverse are probably best described as 'alternative,' particularly in its encouragement of new writing talent, but there's a lot more to this venue than a few over-intellectual plays with lots of sweating and swearing. With an excellent bar and a great restaurant for your pre-show meals, The Traverse is its own night out. Even if the cultural side of The Traverse is a bit too much for you for one evening, the on-site bar's still rocking. Otherwise you could just traverse the road and find somewhere else. Get it? Traverse the road? Ok, that was really poor.

🕒 *Box office, Mon–Sat, 10am–6pm;*
Sun, 4pm–8pm

MUSEUMS

Dean Gallery
73 Belford Road
(0131) 624 6200

A stone's throw away from the Modern Art Gallery, the Dean Gallery is just over the road, and free as well. Home to a large amount of work by Edinburgh-born artist Eduardo Paolozzi, which for the uninitiated means loads of huge transformer-like sculptures among other things, it's also pretty good for other exhibitions and has a large Surrealist collection. They have some Picasso as well, who also has paintings just over the road. He gets everywhere that guy.

🕒 *Mon–Sun, 10am–5pm*
🎟 *Free (except*
for special exhibitions)

Museum of Scotland
Chambers Street
(0131) 247 4422

Just up the road from The Royal Museum, The Museum of Scotland, like Ronseal, does exactly what it says on the tin. With everything from burial sites with real skeletons to medieval weaponry, Jacobite jewellery and a full-size steam engine, it charts bonnie Scottieland's history for you in one nicely manageable building. And if you start getting overwhelmed by the fact that you're actually enjoying learning something, just pop up to the rooftop terrace, and hey presto, you get some spectacular views of Edinburgh for nowt.

🕒 *Mon–Sun, 10am–5pm*
🎟 *Free (except for*
special exhibitions)

The Royal Museum

Chambers Street

(0131) 247 4422

If you've ever wondered why animals go extinct, take a look in The Royal Museum. With bears, tigers and walruses all looking severely pissed off that they've been stuffed and put on display, it's a haven for people that love animals. Or hate them, depending on how you look at it. It's also got a Chinese and Japanese collection which includes a real samurai outfit, and it hosts regular special exhibitions. Oh, and there's also an interactive science area for some pretty addictive games – just don't let that cocky little five-year-old beat you.

🕐 *Mon–Sun, 10am–5pm*

💷 *Free (except for special exhibitions)*

The Scottish National Gallery of Modern Art

75 Belford Road

(0131) 624 6200

If you're more avant-garde than old master, then this gallery is definitely worth checking out. They have work by Hockney, Freud and Picasso, so they're up there with the big boys. It's also pretty big – they have 5,000 pieces of work which they have to rotate, 'cos there just ain't enough room for all those paintings. If you want to see something specific, check ahead in case it's one of the days where they're hiding it away. The garden outside is a piece of art in itself, and it cost £380,000 to make. Ouch.

🕐 *Mon–Sun, 10am–5pm*

💷 *Free (except for special exhibitions)*

Out & about

SPORT

Murrayfield Ice Rink

When Itchy first went skating as a wee whipper snapper, an old man held up his half-a-hand and croaked 'If you fall over, make a fist'. As a result, we have all the self control on blades as Tom Cruise does on sofas. Lessons here have helped our fears, but we still prefer our drinks to be the only thing on ice – handily, there's a café to chill out in.

☻ *Standard sessions; Mon–Sun, 2.30pm–4.30pm, £4; Wed, 7.30pm–9.30pm, £3.50; Disco sessions; Fri, 7.30pm–10.30pm, £5; Sat, 7.30pm–10pm, £4; Leisure sessions; Mon, Wed & Fri, 5pm–7pm, £3.50; UK Learn to Skate; Sun, 12pm–1.45pm, £4*
☻ *Skate hire £1–£1.50*

TOURIST ATTRACTIONS

Princes Street Gardens

Feeling a little worn out after all that non-stop shopping 'til you drop on Princes Street? Luckily for you, many years back, those kind founders of Edinburgh planted an unimaginatively-titled garden running parallel to the main high street. Based right in the heart of the city, you've got the attractive bits of Edinburgh in a nutshell on view. You can see the castle, Old Town, New Town, and several monuments, and all without leaving your bench. Oh, and best of all it's seasonal too – the cold months bring with them a popular ice rink and the Winter Wonderland, while national touring bands often choose it as a gig location in the summer.

Royal Botanic Gardens

Inverleith Row

(0131) 552 7171

Not just one for the horticulturally-inclined, and home to all manner of exotic, unusual and beautiful plants for your viewing pleasure. If you're up for something a touch more touristy then you'll love the guided tours; if not, you can find the perfect antidote to the day's stress by merrily frolicking among the pretty flowers. And even if all that gets boring, there are plenty of events, exhibitions, and activities available all year round to keep you firmly entertained.

☻ *Mon–Sun, 10am–4pm (Nov–Feb); 10am–7pm (Apr–Sep); 10am–6pm (Mar & Oct), free entry; glasshouses, £3–£3.50; tours available at 11am and 2pm, £3.50–£4*

The Meadows

Probably the only place in Edinburgh where you're bound to see something new every time you walk by. Stroll through the on an average day and you might see jugglers, picnickers, or the hardcore training sessions of your friendly university Ultimate Frisbee team; come the summer, you'll find it plays host to all kinds of unique Fringe events. As with many things in life though, you kind of have to take the rough with the smooth as far as the Meadows are concerned, and it's not exactly the safest place in Edinburgh. We don't want to be scaremongers or anything and it is getting better, but the area's notorious for its after-dark perils so be sure to watch yourself when making your way through at night.
🕒 *Daily, 24 hours*

Edinburgh Castle

Look up. A bit to your right. There you go, you've found it. The worst choice possible for anyone playing I spy, anyone who's been in Edinburgh for any length of time beyond a three minutes 25 seconds onward connection in Waverley station will know about the castle. We'll grant you it's not the cheapest outing in the world, and paying for the audio guides is like rubbing salt and lime into the shotgun wound of the hefty initial entrance fee, but it provides some of the best views in Edinburgh, and the castle itself is pretty interesting as well. Plus if you come to Edinburgh and don't visit it, people will probably point at you and laugh.
🕒 *Mon–Sun, 9.30am–5.15pm*
💰 *£9.50*

30🕒...29🕒...28🕒...27🕒...26🕒...25🕒...24🕒...23🕒...22🕒

Half an hour of fun

So you have 30 minutes to kill and you don't just want to stand around pretending you're texting someone. Pop into **The Royal Museum** (Chambers Street, 0131 247 4422) or **The National Gallery of Scotland** (The Mound, 0131 624 6200), where the main exhibitions are all free. Otherwise go and sit somewhere warm. **Biblos** (Chambers Street, 0131 226 7177), **Chocolate**

Soup (Hunter Square, 0131 225 7669) and the delightful **Beanscene** (Holyrood Road, 0131 557 6541) are all good places to escape the relentless Edinburgh weather for a bit. If it's sunny (ahem...), then go for a stroll. **The Botanic Gardens** are unlikely to disappoint. If you're lucky you might even find some pretty flowers which you can smell at your leisure. Delightful.

🕒8...🕒6...🕒10...🕒11...🕒12...🕒13...🕒14...🕒15...🕒16

Out & about

Edinburgh Festival Fringe

180 High Street (Box office)

(0131) 226 0026

This year there were over 28,000 performances at the Edinburgh Fringe. That's more people than Peter Stringfellow thinks he's had sex with. Next year will no doubt be just as good, with late-night drinking, loads of good comedy and theatre, some all-important celeb-spotting and pissing in public all in full force. Loads of new up-and-coming talent plus some established names who just quite like coming back every year, The Edinburgh Fringe Festival is probably the best thing you can experience in Edinburgh. It's on for a whole month as well, so it's actually extraordinarily difficult to miss.

ⓞ *5th–27th August 2007*

Edinburgh Tattoo

32 Market Street

(08707) 555 118

During the Edinburgh Festival you'll probably have a minor heart attack around about 10pm every evening. Don't worry though, it's not the start of the apocalypse to end all humankind, it's just those people at the castle letting loose with some bad-ass fireworks after the Military Tattoo. Featuring brave regiments from all over the world, they march around in formation and dazzle you with their organisational abilities. Fear their perfectly synchronised marching. A big hit every year and on every night, the Military Tattoo is to the Edinburgh Festival what pickle is to cheese. A nice accompaniment but not essential.

ⓞ *3rd–25th August 2007*

Stag & hen

Illustration by Thomas Denbigh

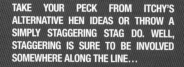

TAKE YOUR PECK FROM ITCHY'S ALTERNATIVE HEN IDEAS OR THROW A SIMPLY STAGGERING STAG DO. WELL, STAGGERING IS SURE TO BE INVOLVED SOMEWHERE ALONG THE LINE…

Unless the bride/groom's into the type of swinging that doesn't happen in park play areas (if it does – hell, you need to move to a better estate), by saying 'I do' your friend is promising not to indulge in bratwurst boxing with anyone but their chosen partner. For £52 per person, you can make sure they pack in the porking prior to the big day at a sausage-making course (www.osneylodgefarm.co.uk), and fry up the results the morning after to calm your hangovers.

As they're already selflessly donating themselves to someone else for life, chuck some extra charity in the mix; if you can raise enough cash for a good cause, experiences like bungee jumping, fire walking and skydiving are absolutely free. Wedding guests could pledge sponsorship as part of their gifts to the couple, and the money saved could go towards an extra few days on the honeymoon. Suitable charities for those getting hitched to munters include the Royal National Institute of the Blind or Battersea Dogs' Home.

IF YOU'RE AFTER GUILTY PLEASURES, WHY NOT GO FOR THE OLD CLASSICS? NO, NOT PROSTITUTION AND PICKING YOUR SCABS, BUT CHEESE AND VOMIT

Under cover of night and with a well-picked disguise, there's no reason you can't go to a crappy club and have a good time. You know the ones: neon-coloured booze, *Summer of '69* blaring in your ears, some deranged Scotsman gnawing on your shoulder when you're queuing at the bar – the usual. **Lava/Ignite** (3 West Toll Cross, 0131 228 3252) is the quintessential club that's a complete hole and yet still manages to be enjoyable. Providing you take advantage of their cheap drinks deals. Otherwise the smell of vomit might just push you over the edge.

Alternatively there's **Stereo** (28 Kings Stables Road, 0131 229 7986). You have to be pretty brave to come here, and there's a chance that Tuesday night's Shagtag might just prove too dirty even for the most sordid of you, but it's worth a look anyway. Now be gone young ones, but just make sure you remember that Itchy isn't responsible for who you take home.

Guilty
pleasures

Illustration by Si Clark
www.si-clark.co.uk

Laters

Laters

Late-night Shopping

One way to avoid the queues for the checkout. And Itchy has been known to use a deserted changing room for all sorts. Nobody's going to notice. Ocean Terminal (0131 555 8888, Ocean Drive, Leith) is open 'til 8pm on weekdays, as is Kinnaird Retail Park (0870 010 2030, Newcraighill Road), though it's pretty far out. It's late-night shopping on Thursdays, when many of the shops are open 'til 7pm or 8pm, and a few book shops like Bookworld (0131 225 3192, 63 Princes Street) are open 'til 11pm on weekdays. In case you feel like a late-night read.

Late-night drinking

God bless the late pub closing times in Edinburgh. Every single bar in the city is open 'til 1am most nights, so you're not going to get kicked out at 11pm like those poor sods across the border. Then there are some bars/clubs open 'til 3am if you're still hankering for some dirty mixers and cocktails. Try Prive Council (Hanover Street, 0131 225 8808) or Medina (45-47 Lothian Street, 0131 225 6313) for a cheeky late-night bevvy, or give Garibaldi's (97a Hanover Street, 0131 220 3007) a look. Everyone knows that the Mexicans enjoy a drink or two. What could possibly go wrong?

After-hours food shopping

You can head down to the Sainsbury's at Cameron Toll (6 Lady Road, 0131 666 2777) any time before 10pm. If 10pm sounds too early, and you're more worried about the midnight munchies or the 3am… whatever they ares, then try Asda at The Jewel, (3 Newmarket Road, 0131 669 9151) or else Tesco in Corstophine, (30 Meadow Place, 0845 677 9193). They're both open 24 hours, and there are offers everywhere. Just remember that getting 20 packs of Jaffa Cakes for the price of ten isn't necessarily the outstanding idea it seems after fifteen pints.

Food now!

The person you're walking home with at 3am is talking some crap about their dog, and all you can think about is food. Dario's (85 Lothian Road, 0131 228 4193) is good for late-night pizza, and lets you sit around 'til 3am or so. Pizza Express (32 Queensbury Street, 0131 225 8863) is generously open 'til midnight, and there are plenty of other takeaways around. There's even a McDonalds (137 Princes Street) which is open really late on Fridays and Saturdays. So there's your food situation sorted. Sadly we can't sort out your mate's endless drivel though.

Post-club action

If you're up in Edinburgh during the Festival, or for Hogmanay, then you'll be delighted to know that most places are open 'til 3am thanks to special late licences. And if you want to hit a club afterwards, they'll usually be open 'til about 5am. The good city of Edinburgh is even generous enough to provide you with a pub called The Penny Black (17 West Register Street, 0131 556 1106) which opens at 6am. It's quite likely you'll be sharing a pint with a group of postmen before they start on their rounds. 24-hour bingeing has never been so easy. Hurrah for responsible drinking.

Gasping for a cigarette

Are you finding that your breathing isn't quite as restricted as it usually is? Almost as if your lungs are functioning normally? Don't worry, a cigarette will have you wheezing again in no time. Late night petrol stations are always a bit of a saviour for fags at 4am, as is Canonmills (23 Canonmills, 0131 556 0642), which is open 24/7 and will sort you out with those Camels in no time. Alternatively, if it's just the one you need to put you back on track, you could always just try and scab a cigarette off a random passer-by. Simply use your gypsy good looks and that winning smile.

LC05 FNZ • LC05 FNZ • LC05 FNZ • LC05 FNZ • LC05 FNZ

Late licences

If you're in Edinburgh for the Festival, which, let's face it, every self-respecting human being should be, then finding places *without* a late licence is the real challenge. The rest of the year, you'll have to look that little bit harder. A good place to start is **Negociants** (45–47 Lothian Street, 0131 225 6313), which is open 'til 3am every night, and serves decent food until 2.30am.

So you can enjoy a nice sit-down meal and a mojito while your contemporaries have kebab sauce dripping down their chops. Or there's the splendid **Teviot** (Bristo Square, 0131 650 4673) where the bar's cheap and open 'til 3am. Or just go all out and pop along to a nightclub. It'll seem like a bad idea at work the next morning, but it'll sure be fun while it lasts.

LC05 FNZ • LC05 FNZ • LC05 FNZ • LC05 FNZ • LC05 FNZ

Laters

X-rated entertainment

Some nights, going to the trouble of chatting someone up, getting to know them and suchlike, all just seems too much of an effort. Being witty, charming and funny all at once while trying to keep your gaze focused on their face can be a bit of a struggle, but luckily there are plenty of strip clubs around where women will take their clothes off for you. You just need to give them a bit of money. Try the infamous Pubic Triangle, which comprises of strip clubs and 'saunas'. Ahem. Find it in between Tollcross, Lothian Road and The Grassmarket. Just follow those bright lights and gawp away.

Late-night entertainment

If you like to watch a good fight, then all you need to do for after-hours kicks is to hang around the Lothian Road on a Friday or Saturday night. Looking for a more mellow evening? Head to one of the cinemas, with Cineworld (130 Dundee Street, 0871 200 2000) and Ocean Terminal (0131 555 8888, Ocean Drive, Leith) both hosting late-night showings. For indie films, try The Cameo (38 Home Street, 0131 228 4141). Alternatively, you can always wait until August, when the number of late-night comedy shows will mean that you're never stuck for entertainment.

Fun @ night

DON'T WASTE THE GIFT OF INSOMNIA BY COUNTING IMAGINARY ANIMALS – GO CREATE SOME SHEAR (ARF) MAYHEM IN THE EARLY AM AND ENTER THE ITCHY TWILIGHT ZONE. WE WOOL IF YOU WOOL

Go jousting – First up, feed up for some insane-sbury's prices. As witching hours approach, 24-hour supermarkets reduce any unsold fresh produce to mere coppers; pick up a feast for a few pauper's pennies and buy them clean out of 10p French sticks, which are spot on for sword fights. Up the ante by jousting using shopping trolleys or bicycles in place of horses, or start a game of ciabatta-and-ball by bowling a roll.

Play street games – Take some chalk to sketch a marathon hopscotch grid down the entire length of the thoroughfare, or an anaconda-sized snakes and ladders board writhing across your town square. Break the trippy silence and deserted stillness of the dead shopping areas with a tag, catch or British bulldog competition, and be as rowdy as you like – there's no-one around to wake.

Play Texaco bingo – Alternatively, drive the cashier at the all-night petrol station honey nut loopy by playing Texaco bingo: the person who manages to make them go back and forth from the window the most times to fetch increasingly obscure, specific and embarrassing items wins. Along with your prize-winning haul of mango chutney-flavoured condoms, Tena Lady towelettes and tin of eucalyptus travel sweets, be sure to pick up a first-edition paper to trump everyone over toast with your apparently psychic knowledge of the day ahead's events-to-be. Whatever you do, remember: you snooze, you lose.

Illustration by Thomas Denbigh

Book cut-price, last minute accommodation with Itchy Hotels

Itchy Hotels has a late booking database of over 500,000 discount hotel rooms and up to 70% off thousands of room rates in 4-star and 5-star hotels, bed and breakfasts, guesthouses, apartments and luxury accommodation in the UK, Ireland, Europe and worldwide.

hotels.itchycity.co.uk
or book by phone: 0870 478 6317

Sleep

Sleep

SWANKY

The Balmoral Hotel
1 Princes Street
(0131) 556 2414

That'll be one arm and one leg please. It might be the most expensive place in town, but it's also definitely the best.

Double rooms, from £160 per person

Sheraton Grand Hotel and Spa
1 Festival Square
(0131) 229 9131

If the prices at the Balmoral make you want to weep into your pillow, the Sheraton will only make you want to shed the odd tear. Still the first word in luxury though.

Double rooms, from £85 per person

MID-RANGE

Acorn Guest House
70 Pilrig Street
(0131) 554 2187

Acorn Guest House is a gay-friendly guest house with only five bedrooms. These two facts are unconnected.

Double rooms, from £25 per person

Best Western Edinburgh Capital Hotel
187 Clermiston Road
(0131) 535 9988

The best hotel in the west of the city, and slightly cheaper than the top hotels. Still, it's not the most sensible choice for those on a shoestring...

Double rooms, from £49.50 per person

Dunstane House
4 West Coates
(0131) 337 6169

If Sherlock Holmes had existed, then he most probably would have stayed here, because his mother's maiden name was Dunstane. You'll be thanking Itchy if it helps you win a pub quiz.

Double rooms, from £49 per person

Old Waverley Hotel
43 Princes Street
(0131) 556 4648

Back in the day this used to attract all the early trainspotters, as it's right next to Waverley station. It also means that it's a pretty forgivingly short walk to your hotel if you get the train in.

Double rooms, from £49 per person

CHEAP

Braveheart House

26 Gilmore Place

(0131) 221 9192

If you can resist the urge to quote lines from the film, then this is a nice, cosy little B&B with a personal touch.

🛏 *Rooms, from £20 per person*

Brodies Backpackers Hostel

93 High Street

(0131) 556 6770

Despite all the 'gnarly' anecdotes about mundane travelling experiences you're likely to hear here, Brodies is so cheap that you won't mind in the slightest. Why not make up a few stories of your own?

🛏 *Beds, from £9 per person*

Edinburgh Backpackers

16 Fleshmarket Close

(0131) 220 2200

Yes, this hotel is on THE Fleshmarket close that Ian Rankin was talking about when he wrote the book of the same name. So now you know. The Backpackers is a cracking place to grab a cheap night's kip.

🛏 *From £15 per person*

Smart City Hotels

50 Blackfriars Street

(0870) 892 3000

Really smart, this hotel, and really cheap too. Don't expect welcoming mints on your pillow or free toiletries that you can 'borrow' after your stay, but do expect to have money left over to fully enjoy Edinburgh.

🛏 *Twin rooms, from £12 per person*

City Centre Guest House & Hostel

87 Shandwick Place

(0131) 221 1991

If you want something a bit more personal, then City Centre Guest House is a good alternative. You'll even get change from a tenner for your trouble.

🛏 *From £9 per person*

Cowgate Tourist Hostel

94–116 Cowgate

(0131) 226 2153

Don't you hate tourists? You know, with their weird sandal/white sock combos and their continual map consultations. Well here's the hotel where they're all kept. Feel free to join them.

🛏 *From £12 per person*

Useful info

Useful info

BEAUTY

Bannatynes

43 Queen Street

(0131) 225 8384

Gym, pool, spa, aerobics studio. In fact, just about everything you need for a beauty fix.

© Mon–Fri, 6.30am–8pm;

Sat–Sun, 8am–8pm

Zen Lifestyle

9 Bruntsfield Place

(0131) 477 3535

Feeling a bit ugly? Well with the nail extensions, safe tan, slimming treatments, CACI, waxing and massage on offer here, there's absolutely no reason you should go on suffering.

© Mon–Fri, 8am–10pm; Sat–Sun, 9am–6pm

Celeste Beauty Spa

1–1a Leven Street

(0131) 221 1900

You're going to the ball. You've got your dress, your shoes, your hair and your Prince Charming sorted. All you need to do now is get yourself down to Celeste for a full makeover.

© Mon–Fri, 9am–8pm; Sat, 9am–6pm

TATTOO

Liquid Ink Tattoos

Downstairs in Flip, 59–61 South Bridge

(0131) 558 8801

Just met the love of your life? Why not get their name inked on your chest?

© Mon–Sat, 10.30am–5pm

€ From £25

MALE HAIRDRESSERS

Barbers 321

3 Clerk Street, (0131) 668 3666

© Mon–Sat, 9am–6pm

€ From £7

York Barbers

4b York Place, (0131) 558 7303

© Mon–Fri, 9am–5pm; Thu, 9am–6pm;

Sat, 10am–3pm

€ From £7

UNISEX HAIRDRESSERS

Boosh

307 Cowgate, (0131) 556 9993

© Mon, Wed & Fri, 10am–6pm;

Tue & Thu 10am–8pm; Sat, 9am–4pm

€ From £27

Charlie Miller

13 Stafford Street

(0131) 226 5550

© Mon–Fri, 9am–5.30pm;

Thu, 9am–6.30pm; Sat, 8.30am–5pm;

€ From £25

Cheynes

45a York Place

(0131) 558 1010

© Mon–Fri, 9am–8pm; Sat–Sun, 9am–5pm

€ From £20

Supercuts

St James Centre, Old Town

(0131) 557 5259

© Mon–Sat, 9am–4.45pm; Thu, 9am–5.54pm

€ From £11.95

BUSES

Lothian Buses
(0131) 555 6363
A bit like cars, but bigger, and more people.

National Express
(0131) 555 6363
Leaving home for ever? Take the bus!

TOURIST INFORMATION

Scotland Information Centre
(08452) 255 121

TRAVEL INFORMATION

Traveline
(08706) 082 608

TRAINS

First Scotrail
(08457) 550 033
The best way to get a change of scenery.

GNER
(08457) 225 225
Need to leave Scotland fast? Get on a GNER train. No questions asked.

National Rail Enquiries
(08457) 484 950
Any train, any time, anywhere. Err, almost.

PLANES

Edinburgh Airport
(0131) 333 1000

TAXIS

Central Taxis
(0131) 299 2468

City Cabs
(0131) 228 1211

K2 Cabs
(0131) 229 7373

Radiocabs
(0131) 225 9000

Sky Cab
(0131) 344 3344

Starcab
(0131) 554 9994

Useful info

TAKEAWAY CHINESE

Inspiration Oriental
10 Commercial Street
(0131) 555 6708
Be inspired today. And not in a poetic sense. Give these guys a call asap.
🕒 *Mon–Fri, 11am–11pm;*
Sat–Sun, 12pm–11pm

Sesame Chinese Takeaway
230a Portobello High Street
(0131) 669 8721
Sadly Big Bird doesn't come to deliver your food, and ze Count will not be along to help you rummage through your small change when it comes to the bill. But it's still Chinese, and it's still good.
🕒 *Mon–Sun, 4.30pm–12am*

TAKEAWAY CURRY

Bangalore
52 Home Street
(0131) 229 1348
Get the nice people at Bangalore to make you a curry and set your world alight. And possibly your throat. And backside.
🕒 *Sun–Sat, 5pm 'til late*

Kasbah
24 Marchmont Road
(0131) 229 2001
If you're thinking of rocking the proverbial Kasbah, this is the place for it. That doesn't mean smashing the place up, it means ordering a nice Indian takeaway and a classy Belgian beer or two.
🕒 *Mon–Sun, 5pm–11pm*

FISH AND CHIPS

Kingfisher Takeaway
69–71 Bread Street
(0131) 229 3028
It's a hard life for fish. They spend their short lives in a freezing sea, before being caught, battered and fried in oil. Poor buggers.
🕒 *Mon–Sun, 12.30pm–1.30am*

TAKEAWAY KEBABS

Kebab Express
252 Gorgie Road
(0131) 337 9070
Let's be honest. After twelve pints of lager, there's absolutely nothing like tepid lamb served with salad and slathered in sauce.
🕒 *Fri–Sat, 4.30pm 'til late*

TAKEAWAY PIZZA

Dario's Pizza
85–87 Lothian Road
(0131) 229 9625
You eat it when you're drunk, and cold for breakfast the next day, and then you realise why pizza is the greatest thing ever created.
🕒 *Mon–Sun, open 'til 4am*

Mamma's American Pizza Co
139 Bruntsfield Place
(0131) 229 7008
Sure it's expensive, but then you're not getting dough that's been soaked in fat for 10 minutes and then had some grated cheese scattered on it. This is proper pizza, big as you like, made before your very eyes.
🕒 *Mon–Sun, 12pm–11pm*

Support

Illustration by Joly Braime

Nightline

Anonymous and confidential support and
information service
(0131) 557 4444

Police

Lothian and Borders Police, Fettes Avenue
(0131) 311 3131

Accident & Emergency

Royal Infirmary of Edinburgh, Old Dalkeith Road
(0131) 536 1000

Doctor

Broughton Health Clinic, 57a Albany Street
(0131) 556 1586

NHS Dentist

Edinburgh Dental Institute, 1 Lauriston Place
(0131) 536 4900

Family Planning

Dean Terrace Centre
18 Dean Terrace
(0131) 332 7941

Rape Helpline

(0131) 556 9437

The Samaritans

(0131) 221 9999

Fire and Rescue

Lothian and Borders
Fire Brigade Headquarters,
Lauriston Place
(0131) 228 2401

Frank

Drugs Helpline
(0800) 776 600

www.itchyedinburgh.co.uk

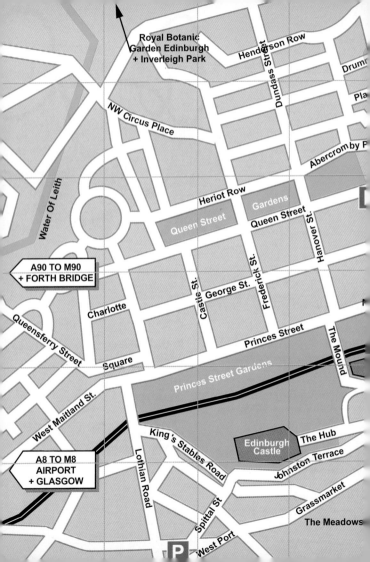

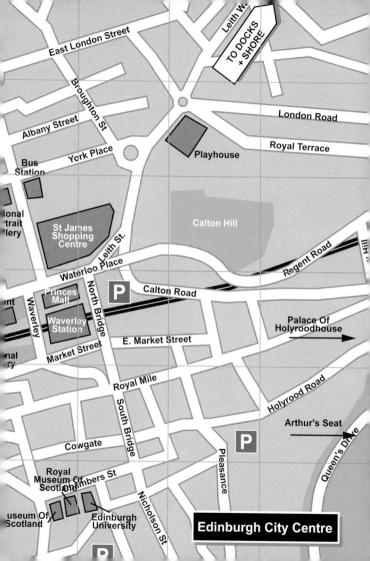

Index

Gazing at the stars

THERE'S NOTHING LIKE A GOOD CELEB SPOT TO MAKE YOUR DAY SEEM MORE EXCITING, SO HERE'S A RUNDOWN OF WHO YOU'RE LIKELY TO SEE IN EDINBURGH

Daniel Craig may be the new Bond, but **Sean Connery** is surely the most iconic. He was born in Edinburgh, and worked as a milkman for Scotmid before stardom beckoned. You can even see the place where he lived, marked by a tiny plaque on a gate near Fountainbridge. Nowadays he's been replaced by **J.K. Rowling**, the creator of the world's most famous wizard. If you hang around Morningside, and sit around in nice coffee houses all afternoon, you may be lucky enough to see her. Don't bother asking her how the last book ends though, as she won't say anything.

Then there's the Edinburgh Fringe Festival. Not so much a case of celebrity stalking as inadvertent spotting. If you hang around **The Pleasance Courtyard** or **Bristo Square**, you won't go five minutes without spotting some famous comedian or TV personality. At last year's Fringe, Itchy became pretty convinced that squinty, gay, American comedian Scott Capurro was stalking us round the streets of Edinburgh. Wherever we went, he'd show up five minutes later, even going as far as booking himself a convenient slot on the line up of whatever show we were watching. Seriously, Scott, get over it – we're not interested.